You want a *WHAT* for a Pet?!

A GUIDE TO 12 ALTERNATIVE PETS

by Betsy Sikora Siino

HOWELL
BOOK
HOUSE

Howell Book House
A Simon & Schuster Macmillan Company
1633 Broadway
New York, NY 10019-6785

Book design by Kris Tobiassen

Library of Congress Cataloging-in-Publication Data

Sikora-Siino, Betsy.

You want a want for a pet?! : a guide to 12 alternative pets / by Betsy Sikora Siino.

p.   cm.

ISBN: 0-87605-485-8

1. Pets.   I. Title.   II. Title: Alternative pets

SF413.S52   1996

636.088'7--dc20   96-5610

                                                              CIP

CONTENTS

ACKNOWLEDGMENTS

I am deeply indebted to countless individuals who have contributed both directly and indirectly to the accuracy of this book.

In my career as a writer and journalist with an unwavering focus on animals of all kinds, my goal has always been to report with accuracy for the well-being of my subjects. I could not accomplish this without the talented journalists and authors whose books and articles I have read through the years, and the many dedicated veterinarians, researchers, breeders and enthusiasts with whom my work has brought me in contact. All of them, somewhere along the way, have contributed their passions and experiences to this present work.

I thank all the countless named and unnamed herpetologists, breeders and pet owners who have so willingly discussed exotic pet care with me through the past year. Among these are David Keune, Nicole Vollmer, Keli O'Brien, Keith and May Walsh, Dr. Donna Nykaza of Lincolnway Animal Hospital in Illinois, and my colleagues Kathleen Etchepare, Russ Case, Phillip Samuelson and Kathleen Wood, all of whom enthusiastically volunteered their opinions (and sometimes their animals) for the enrichment of this work.

For their insight into amphibians and hermit crabs, thanks go to Bill Pierce of Glades Herp and Don Salomon of Brelean Corporation, respectively. I similarly thank California potbellied pig breeder Karen Milojevich for her enthusiastic discussions about her beloved pig friends. The same must be said for hedgehog breeder Dawn Wrobel of Ain't No Creek Ranch in Illinois, and "rat ladies" Debbie Ducommun (of the Rat Fan Club) and Kelle Steward (of the American Fancy Rat and Mouse Association).

I offer much appreciation, as well, for the information gathered from the Southwestern Herpetologists Society; the National Committees on Potbellied Pigs; the American Fancy Rat and Mouse Association; the Rat Fan Club; the American Rat, Mouse and Hamster Society; the North American

Hedgehog Association; the California Domestic Ferret Association and the California Turtle and Tortoise Club.

A special note of appreciation must go to Robert Gale Breene III, PhD, who volunteered much time and effort to ensure that, for the well-being of big hairy spiders everywhere, the tarantula chapter of this book would meet the high standards of the American Tarantula Society. Similar appreciation goes to dedicated spider breeders and caretakers Mark and Rhonda Hart of West Coast Zoological in San Deigo, California, who introduced me personally to the exotic beauty of the tarantula.

Special thanks, as well, to python breeders David and Tracy Barker of Vida Preciosa International Inc. in Boerne, Texas (co-authors, along with Philippe de Vosjoli and Roger Klingenberg, DVM, of *The Ball Python Manual*). I found priceless their expertise in the care of reptiles and amphibians (and Dave's absolutely breathtaking photographs of these animals); their passion for snakes, frogs, toads and salamanders; and their ability to make one want to run right out and buy a python.

And, finally, I thank the animals. Without their inspiration, I could not have written a word.

INTRODUCTION

Tarantulas. Snakes. Rats. You want a *what* for a pet!?

Yes it's true. Just as the title of this book implies, there are people among us who do crave a big hairy spider, a slithery serpent or a long-tailed rodent as a pet. No, these animals are not ideal for every circumstance or every pet owner, but they are gaining an increasingly strong following, often facilitated by our ever-increasing urban sprawl and the resulting cramped "no pets allowed" living situations into which we are thrust.

ODDLY APPEALING

For people who find themselves faced with such restrictions, yet who also simply cannot conquer that nagging desire to live with animals, an alternative pet species, one that is clean, quiet and need not be walked every day, may just be the answer. On the other hand, some pet owners have a natural hankering for a pet that requires even more supervision and attention than does a cat or a dog. These people, too, can find satisfaction in an alternative pet, perhaps a ferret or a potbellied pig.

But there is a downside to these relationships that so often begin with such hope, enthusiasm and good intentions. That downside is rooted in impulse and ignorance. Never should any pet be purchased on an impulse, especially a pet about which the prospective owner has very little knowledge or understanding.

TOO OFTEN DISPOSED

Consider, for example, the quandary that faces reptiles. Within the pages of this book, you will be meeting several of this family: the green iguana, turtles and tortoises, and the very popular ball python. Interest in reptile pets is burgeoning, yet the public's knowledge regarding their care does not seem to be keeping up, evident in the number of reptiles that meet premature deaths in the hands of well-meaning or negligent owners, or that wind up at animal shelters.

Proper care, which is what this book is all about, relies not on assumptions and hearsay, but on solid research, preferably begun before the new pet is brought into the household. Only when the commitment—and all pets require a commitment—required for the care of a particular pet is understood, can an intelligent decision on whether or not that animal would make a proper addition to a particular household be made.

The bottom line? Don't buy on impulse. You may be tempted to do so, perhaps because of a current trend, or, as often happens with reptiles and amphibians, because a prospective pet seems so easy to care for. Only after you take the plunge do you discover that the animal involves a great deal of care that you may or may not be willing or able to provide.

KNOW WHAT YOU'RE GETTING INTO

There is no such thing as a no-maintenance pet. Just because a salamander, a tortoise or a mouse is quiet and resides in a terrarium or a cage, does not mean that animal doesn't require care and attention. On the other hand, such pets and their care regimens can be very addictive and feed our desires to commune with nature. Just ask anyone who begins the adventure with a single bullfrog or garter snake, and soon finds his or her home filled with tanks of exotic tropical reptiles and amphibians, each housed in a habitat that simulates what it would have in the wild. Life for such individuals becomes a never-ending quest to increase their knowledge and to provide the resident pets with everything they need to remain content and healthy.

The greatest fear for any true enthusiast is popularity of a particular pet species. Whenever a pet becomes popular, as has happened with the green iguana, it inevitably leads to trouble. Thousands of animals are acquired for reasons other than an individual's true desire to live with them and to commit to their long-term care. Neophytes often underestimate how much a young iguana, python or potbellied pig is going to grow (and unethical sellers may be less-than-anxious to discuss it). By the time the owner realizes this, the initial excitement and novelty have worn off. What then becomes of the animal?

The moral of the story is to choose a pet because you are truly compelled to live with such a creature and you are confident it can thrive within your lifestyle. Buy on a whim because of a trend or a desire to impress, and you won't be sufficiently motivated to provide the animal with the proper long-term care and attention it needs and deserves.

Legalities can be another obstacle. A great many species today—an example being many members of the tortoise family—are endangered, meaning, for the most part, that they may not be kept as pets. Take one in, and it may be confiscated somewhere down the line. Some states, too, enforce their own restrictions. While, for example, you may be able to keep a ferret or a hedgehog in one state, they are off limits in others, so find out ahead of time.

Another consideration is the issue of captive-bred and farm-raised animals versus wild-caught specimens. This is a major subject of debate with reptiles and amphibians, and most agree that given the current climate, captive-breeding is the wave of the future. Experts are becoming increasingly successful at breeding exotic animals in captivity, and many further believe that a captive-bred snake or frog makes a better pet. Furthermore, many owners of captive-bred animals feel more comfortable knowing that their animals were bred specifically as pets rather than for life in the wild.

PARTICULAR PETS, PARTICULAR NEEDS

With these broader issues explored, you may proceed onward to an investigation of the everyday details of the animal's care. Some species, for example, have dietary requirements that make many a prospective owner squeamish. A snake that must consume whole mice and a frog's taste for live insects are not ideal for everyone. Don't assume that you will be able to coerce the animal into subsisting on a different food which you are more comfortable feeding. To believe you can is to disrespect and disregard the animal's needs.

While some of the animals in this book are considered so-called "easy-care" pets, they, like any pet, will not thrive on neglect. As a rule of thumb, with the exception of the newly fed ball python, none of these animals should be left alone for longer than a weekend (even that may be too long for the gregarious potbellied pig). All require routine home care, even when their families are on vacation.

What many people do not realize is that there are pet sitters for these types of animals, just as there are for dogs, cats and other pets. Talk to other owners or to veterinarians to find someone reliable and knowledgeable.

Equally critical is an investigation into the prospective pet's housing needs. You must fully understand the type of accommodations required to allow the animal to thrive, whether that be a tank for an aquatic turtle, a ferret-proof living room for a rambunctious ferret or a large outdoor enclosure for a potbellied pig. Learn how to clean the habitat, for an allegiance to impeccable hygiene also plays a critical role in the commitment. Regular cleaning will help foster longevity and contentment, help prevent disease and keep the odor inherent to some exotic species under control.

Once you have made an informed decision of the right exotic pet, you enter the next step of the equation: determining where to obtain this animal and how to select a healthy specimen. Information on selecting a healthy pet will be covered in detail in the chapters that follow, but selecting a reputable source from which to obtain one is the same for all pet species, and it does require some legwork.

KNOW WHERE TO SHOP FOR YOUR PET

While a general pet store may be a fine source for a hermit crab or a pair of mice, you may be better off seeking reptiles and amphibians at shops that specialize in those animals. Their staffs are usually better informed about the animals' care because they are often reptile or amphibian hobbyists themselves.

Breeders are another excellent source for healthy captive-bred reptiles and amphibians, and the best source when you are seeking such animals as ferrets and potbellied pigs, animals whose temperaments and future adaptability as pets hinge on early socialization. Don't forget local animal shelters, either. Sadly, exotic pets are on their way to becoming as common in shelters as cats and dogs, and many a fine iguana, ferret, tortoise or even snake can be found at shelters these days.

Regardless of the source, make sure the facility is clean and the breeder or staff members knowledgeable. Beware of sellers who insist that this animal is perfect for you, perfect for everyone. If, on the other hand, they ask you about your lifestyle and your own knowledge about the animals you are interested in, and encourage you to ask questions, consider that a very good sign.

Ethical, concerned breeders or sellers of exotic pets will speak most about the animal's well-being and what you can do to ensure it lives the most rewarding life possible. They are pleased to answer your questions with clear, concise answers, and may even be visibly relieved to see that you are taking such an active role in learning as much as possible about your prospective pet. Breeders with ethics and genuine passion, after all, hope to place their animals in homes where they will remain for the rest of their lives.

Sometimes, even with proper preparation, the relationship between an exotic pet and its owner just doesn't work out. Think ahead about this possibility, and by all means, if this comes to pass, do not release the animal into the wild. Re-releasing even a native salamander or toad collected from a nearby wooded area can introduce disease to the resident wild population. Releasing a domestic ferret, captive-raised iguana or tropical frog into a local forest is not only cruel, but potentially damaging to the local ecosystem.

Non-native pet species released into a foreign environment can die because of a lack of their normal diet, climate and habitat. In their struggle to survive, they can wreak havoc with the local native wildlife, which ultimately will negatively affect the public's perception of these animals as pets. Rather than allow this to happen, a reputable breeder or pet shop will take the animal back in the event of a mismatch.

Exotic pet species are far better off in health and circumstance than they were twenty years ago. Much more has been gleaned about their care requirements, evident in the influx of products and information now available to the public. At the same time, more and more veterinarians are specializing in the care of exotic and non-traditional pets, making their services available to people who want to ensure their pets enjoy the finest health and care.

WORTH THE TROUBLE

While this all sounds like a great deal of preparation to go through, the rewards are immeasurable. Living with a tortoise, a rat, a snake or a tarantula, just like living with a cat or a dog, initiates us into a whole other world. We come to know these pets as individuals, and, whether reptile, amphibian, arachnid or mammal, each individual has a distinct personality, as well as personal tastes in food, sleeping habits and play behaviors.

Any pet we choose to take into our homes, whether it be spider, toad, rodent or lizard, deserves an owner committed to do all he or she can to ensure only the finest care for that pet. None deserve to suffer, but, unfortunately, far too many of these more unusual pets do, primarily because of negligence, and, more commonly, ignorance. That is what this book will hope to remedy.

This is not a breeding manual. Rather, its focus is on keeping non-traditional animals as companions. Yet even when we speak of exotic pets in this light, there are countless opinions on what is correct in regard to proper care. On some issues there is simply no consensus among experts. The majority opinion is often countered by that of equally passionate dissenters. Every attempt in this book has been made to present the marketplace of ideas, resulting in a picture of what will make the animal the most comfortable, the most content and the healthiest in its life with the human species.

A profound sense of satisfaction comes from knowing you have taken a species so unlike your own and committed to its care. How fascinating and rewarding it can be to see your pet thrive and even enjoy a long and contented life with our species, which is not always heralded for its commitments to others. In this way, caring for a pet, any pet, can be a grand and very noble adventure.

The ball python is a beautiful reptile, its skin rivaling the colors and patterns of a leopard. *David G. Barker*

CHAPTER 1

Serpentine Passions: The Ball Python

It takes a special soul to live with a snake. One is usually born with the compulsion. Why?, those not so genetically endowed may ask. In response, those gifted with the passion will reply: Why would you want anything else?

Few animals inspire as much fascination, revulsion and fear as does the snake. We are led to believe from a variety of sources that this animal is to be reviled, that its long, appendageless form is not a natural result of evolution's sculptress, but rather a sentence, a curse, for some named and unnamed transgressions against mankind. We learn to cringe at the sight of snakes and to fear their bite.

But embrace such popular opinions as your own, and you are likely to be blinded to the inherent beauty of this animal. One of the most beautiful of the family of snakes is a constrictor, a python, called the ball python (referred to by its European friends as the royal python).

The ball python's vibrant beauty, its elegance, its relative docility and its manageable size have made it an immensely popular snake species in the pet trade—often to the snake's misfortune. Its unique habits and attractive temperament have led it down the path of misunderstanding in the hands of people who inadvertently misread its signals. But make the effort to clarify those misconceptions, to understand what this snake is telling you, and the ball python can be one of the finest pet species of snake available today.

GETTING TO KNOW THE BALL PYTHON

Mysterious and silent with a beautiful, anything-but-slimy skin, snakes make quiet, odorless pets for people who may not have enough time to meet the

The Ball Python as a Pet

	Light	1	2	3	4	5	Heavy
TIME COMMITMENT				~			
MAINTENANCE Grooming		~					
Feeding					~		
General Clean-Up				~			
SUITABILITY TO CHILDREN Ages Infant-5		~					
Ages 5-10			~				
Over 10					~		
SOCIABILITY				~			
EXPENSE OF KEEPING				~			

demands of a dog, a cat, or even a tortoise or an iguana. With a refined grace of movement and skin patterns that suggest they must have been designed by an artist, they are hardly the incarnation of evil that myth and legend would have us believe.

The ball python is considered one of the more docile members of the constrictor family of snakes. The constrictors are so named for their habit of wrapping themselves around their prey and "constricting" it, therefore killing it, before ingesting it. Unlike some of its larger cousins—the Burmese python coming immediately to mind—the ball python will attain a moderate average length of about four or five feet in captivity. In the wild they may reach or even exceed the six-foot mark. Distinct by its skin patterns, the ball python sports a stunning skin, typically found in interwoven patterns of brown and gold, although variations, such as piebald and albino, also exist.

The ball python's name describes this snake's habit of curling up into a tight ball-like clump whenever it feels threatened or believes it is encountering a prospective predator—a common occurrence in its home regions on the savannas and sparse forests of western Africa. A wild-caught snake should stop this habit in captivity once it realizes it has nothing to fear. But unfortunately, far too many owners mistake the ball response as a sign of docility rather than stress, and thus take the opportunity to overhandle the snake and increase its stress levels, often, as we will see, with dire results.

Despite a reputation for docility, ball pythons and most constrictors are not appropriate for beginning snake hobbyists. Should you discover an inbred compulsion to live with snakes, it's usually best to begin with a smaller, less-complicated species—such as a garter snake or a king snake—docile, easy-care snakes that can provide a graceful entry into the world of the ball python.

Veteran keepers have found the ball python to be an intelligent animal with intensely touch-sensitive skin. Its adaptability helps it to flourish in captivity when in the hands of a knowledgeable caretaker.

UNDERSTANDING YOUR PYTHON

In temperament, the ball python will never be as affectionate and responsive as a dog or a cat, but, of course, if that is the type of pet behavior you are seeking, then a dog or a cat is a better choice of pet. With gentle routine handling, however, and a clear understanding of the snake's body language, it should become rather tame and learn to accept and even enjoy handling.

This is not to say that this docile snake will never bite. Bite it may, so newcomers to snake ownership must prepare themselves mentally for that possibility. If you are of this camp, it may ease your fears to remember that unlike the jaws of a mammal, a snake's jaws are not engineered for chewing or sinking teeth deeply into human flesh. You are more likely to scar from a dog or cat bite than you are from that of a ball python.

As the recipient of this snake's bite, you will feel a quick strike and a brief twinge of pain, which will be followed by a bit of blood, but not as profuse as you might expect. That's about the brunt of it. Wash the relatively superficial puncture wounds with soap and water, treat the wound with an antibiotic ointment and a band-aid, and don't take the event personally. The snake was just being a snake.

The possibility of biting aside, a healthy relationship between snake and owner must be rooted in trust. To earn a python's trust, leave it alone when it is wrapped like a pretzel into a ball, touch it gently when it's not, and always move slowly and avoid rough handling. Be patient and methodical, and ultimately you will be rewarded with a dignified pet content to play its unique role in a relationship of mutual trust with its human owner.

A good relationship between a snake and owner can never occur unless it involves an owner who is educated in the snake's living requirements and is sensitive to its unique outlook on life. Several elements here are frequently cause for alarm among neophyte owners, but, as we shall see, the owner has great power either to alleviate or to foster such problems.

When contemplating the snake, any snake, both pet and wild, think of the disdain with which it is held among so many cultures, and imagine

When properly bred and handled, the ball python thrives in human company and actually enjoys spending time with its owners.
Michael A. Siino

how it must be to live armless and legless in a world of predators, with only a mouth full of teeth to defend yourself. Think of it that way, and we, predators ourselves, realize that we are more dangerous to pythons than they are to us.

EVALUATING THE PET PYTHON CANDIDATE

You get what you pay for. That is the bottom line when choosing a ball python as a pet. This snake has become so popular that the supply, thanks to captive-hatching programs in its African homeland, has led to such a glut in the pet trade that it is not unusual to find them offered at obscenely low prices. But choose a snake that is being practically given away from a questionable background, and you may discover very soon that it is destined for a short lifespan, refuses to eat, has in no way been socialized to handling and is riddled with parasites and/or disease.

The key to the ball python's longevity—and to the best experience in captivity possible—is choosing a pet whose past is clear, who has already proven it will eat willingly (not always a given with this snake that has a reputation for finicky eating habits), and who already seems to be thriving under the care of humans.

First of all, consider the comparison of the captive-bred python and its wild-caught cousin (not to be confused with snakes hatched in captivity from eggs collected from the wild). Acclimating a wild-caught ball python to life with humans is a challenge which only the very experienced should tackle. In the hands of the inexperienced who are apt to misread this docile snake's behavior, the snake will probably starve to death within months. This is a case of starvation brought on by the incredible stress the snake experiences when thrust into the midst of two-legged predators who insist on handling it whenever it curls into a ball for protection.

The captive-bred and raised ball python, on the other hand, can be a fine pet. Today there are breeders throughout the United States who specialize not only in hatching healthy pythons, but also in easing them into a healthy lifestyle that will ensure their longevity and contentment in captivity. The odds that a snake of this background will be a good eater, enjoy handling and be free of disease and/or parasites are high, much higher than they are for a wild-caught specimen, or even one imported from a captive-hatching program. In choosing the captive-bred python, you are also showing support for people who are deeply committed to snakes and the preservation of their kind in the wild.

A reputable source of pet ball pythons, perhaps a breeder or a pet store that handles reptiles exclusively, will be apparent by the staff's willingness to discuss the background of the snakes they have for sale, and their knowledge about these animals' proper care and handling. Be wary of breeders or shop personnel who market them as the perfect pet species of snake. There is no such thing, of course, and while the ball python is a docile, relatively easy-care constrictor, it can have inherent problems that will be magnified when it is in the care of the ignorant or negligent.

Upon locating a source with which you feel comfortable, evaluate the specimen that interests you both visually and by touch. Python breeders David and Tracy Barker, of Boerne, Texas, suggest that prospective owners look for a ball python that exudes good health. For this animal, that means a snake with a rounded, muscular body and a healthy skin free of lumps, pits, wounds or parasites (ticks or mites). When held, the snake should provide the sensation of muscle in your hand, not of cooked spaghetti.

Avoid a snake that holds its head back, has mucus or discharge in or around its nostrils, or that in any way seems to be suffering from a respiratory infection. The same must be said for signs of mouth rot, evident by redness or a "cheesy" substance growing in and around the mouth.

Behavior is another key component in selecting a ball python that will live contentedly within your household for years to come. First, because feeding can be an issue, try to witness the snake taking a meal. This is a strong indicator that it will do just fine with you, as well. If this is not possible— perhaps the snake isn't hungry at the moment—ask if the snake, especially a young snake, has taken at least four meals willingly in a row. This is information that a reputable seller will gladly, and honestly, provide. If this information is not available, you may want to get a guarantee, choose another snake or commit to the proper care necessary (see "Those First Days") for rehabilitating the problem eater.

Evaluate the snake's willingness to be handled, as well. A well-socialized captive-bred snake that has been raised to trust human handling should have no qualms about being held and evaluated by a stranger. If, on the other hand, the snake curls into a ball the moment you look at it, it is a sign that the snake feels stressed and threatened, and, like the problem eater (which this snake may also be), needs some patient convincing to learn to trust human handling. Be honest with yourself. Are you willing and able to work with this latter type of python? If not, seek one more in keeping behaviorally with your expectations.

A FINICKY EATER

If ever a snake were known for having an eating disorder, that snake would have to be the ball python. For some of these snakes, this reputation is deserved, for others completely irrelevant; just which way a snake will go depends on its background and on its owner.

As with any constrictor, it is imperative before choosing this animal as a pet that one understand the ball python's diet, a diet typically consisting of mice and rats. No, a piece of steak or chicken will not suffice. It needs the balance of nutrients only an entire animal can provide; otherwise malnutrition will result.

The problem emerges in that some snakes cannot be convinced to ingest that package of nutrients; hence this species' reputation for being finicky and for imprinting on certain types of food. Again, a snake bred and raised in captivity by conscientious breeders should present no problem, but a wild-caught individual, or one whose experiences with humans have been anything but positive, is another story.

Sometimes the problem is simply that we offer ball pythons foods with which they are unaccustomed. A young snake that was fed gerbils in Africa (or stalked them in the wild), for example, may balk at the unfamiliar scent of a mouse in its midst.

When you first purchase the snake, it is important to learn what it has been accustomed to eating, because you will probably have to continue the tradition for a while. It can take time, and infinite patience, to convince the python to alter its food of choice. This is yet another reason why the captive-bred ball python, which has most likely been raised on mice and rats, makes the superior pet.

Despite where the snake came from, several physical factors can contribute to a ball python's unwillingness to eat. If the temperature is too cool or too hot within its enclosure, the snake's appetite will dwindle, as will its ability to digest its food properly. Parasitic infestations or illness can also affect the desire to eat, as can a sudden change in diet.

Unfortunately, all too often it is the owner who is to blame for the python's refusal to eat. Overhandling of a timid snake, especially one that frequently curls up into that anxiety-caused ball, and failing to balance the heat gradients within the snake's enclosure, will lead to stress. Stress in turn leads to a hunger strike, and a hunger strike leads to starvation.

A ball python caught up in this cycle will probably curl up into a ball rather than strike out and attempt to bite as would its fellow snakes. The owner, in turn, assuming this to be a sign of tameness, will attempt to handle the snake in a misguided attempt to acclimate it to the human in its life, which only serves to throw the appetite more off kilter. In several months, the snake could be dead.

Fasting itself, however, is not unusual or abnormal in ball pythons, another fact that owners must learn if they are to control their own anxiety in the keeping of this unique species. Although it is less commonly seen in captive-bred snakes, some males, upon reaching sexual maturity, have been known to fast for as long as six months, a year, even longer. If your snake is in this mode, it may not be eating, but it will remain healthy, social and rather uninterested in assuming the ball position.

Owners of this healthy fasting snake may still be inclined to panic, but it is the rare animal that will require force feeding. Should force feeding be in order, this complicated procedure is best performed by a veterinarian or experienced reptile keeper. If done incorrectly, it can cause injury to the snake that may equal or exceed the danger presented by a lack of sustenance.

When frightened or stressed, the ball python will wrap itself into, as its name implies, a ball, an act that uninformed handlers may misread as a sign of docility or contentment.
David G. Barker

THOSE FIRST DAYS

The ball python's eating habits and acceptance of its owner can find a strong foundation in the first few days or weeks that the snake comes to join the household. Although you may be anxious at this time to bring the snake directly into the mix of family activities, resist that. Even the well-socialized snake needs some time to get acclimated to the new scents and environment it has been thrust into.

You should set up its enclosure prior to the snake's arrival; it must be fully equipped and ready to welcome its new inhabitant. This means the hiding box is in place, the temperature gradient is correct, the floor is lined with layers of newspaper and the snake has access to a bowl of fresh, clean water for soaking and drinking. Refrain from supplying dinner, however. That comes later.

Experience has taught python breeders David and Tracy Barker that it's best to leave the snake, including the well-socialized, captive-bred snake, alone for at least two weeks, its enclosure kept in a quiet, secluded area of the house. During this time, say the Barkers, there should be no handling of the snake. Just peek in quietly every day to make sure all is well, and to change the water and remove soiled newspaper flooring.

This time of solitude can turn into months for a wild-caught python, which may choose to remain in its hiding box. One day the python will peek its head out as if to say, "Okay, I'm ready." At that point patient experiments with feeding may begin. After four successful feedings in a row, this more difficult snake will probably be just fine.

For our captive-bred friend, however, feeding may begin at the conclusion of those two introductory weeks. Assuming you do not notice a cloudiness over the eyes that indicates skin shedding is imminent, go ahead and feed the snake. Acclimated as it is, it should readily accept the invitation. After it has taken a couple of meals, you may begin handling the animal.

Build up handling time gradually. Employ the same patience you used when introducing the snake to its new household. To hold the snake, wrap one hand gently yet firmly around its neck behind its head, and with the other hand, support the remainder of the body. Do not squeeze, or you can cause injury or fatal internal bruising—not to mention foster a negative association about handling in the snake.

The ball python's successful introduction to the household does not, however, signal an occasion when you can wrap your pet around your neck and take it to town to show off. That day must never come. Although with proper, gentle handling, the snake can learn to tolerate such exhibitions, a great many people in public cannot. The only benefit to the snake is the sunshine, but displayed in public this way, it may just feed the public's fears and lead to an increase in the public's negative opinions about snakes—as well as legislation forbidding the keeping of reptiles, a serious concern among those who keep them.

This is not to say the ball python should not be invited to participate in more private activities. Many a properly acclimated snake has even learned to enjoy hanging out (literally) with their owners while they watch television, and, with careful supervision, playing in the grass in an enclosed backyard.

MYTHS ABOUT FEEDING A PYTHON

There is a great myth surrounding the keeping of snakes. They will not eat, states this myth, unless they are offered live food. One wonders how many people unwilling to keep snakes because of this accepted notion would change their minds if they knew this just isn't true.

In fact, most dedicated herpetologists believe that if a snake is eating live food, it should be weaned of that as soon as possible. A confrontation with a live mouse or rat places the snake in grave danger, as the prey is usually not shy about fighting back.

A better, safer option, and one more acceptable to most humans, is feeding dead mice or rats, either freshly killed by the owner or purchased frozen. The latter is the easiest option, certainly, and with the increase in popularity of reptile pets, frozen rodents are becoming more readily available. (Store them in a non-see-through container to avoid scaring visitors snooping through your freezer.)

The ball python relies on the combination of a highly developed sense of smell and taste, as well as an ability to differentiate temperatures, to locate its prey. Captive-bred animals are usually content with a diet of mice or small rats, although ball pythons have been known to eat other small rodents, such as gerbils and hamsters, as well.

Young snakes, which require more food than do their elders, should be fed once or twice a week, while non-fasting adult snakes usually require sustenance every seven to ten days. Evening is usually the optimum feeding time. A young python should get one young pinky or fuzzy mouse or rat per feeding, an adult two or three adult mice or weanling rats (only larger adult ball pythons should be offered adult rats, and small ones at that). Avoid food items that are substantially larger than the snake's head, and avoid fostering life-threatening obesity by overfeeding.

If you are feeding a frozen mouse or rat, it must be thawed completely before it is offered to the snake. Leaving it out for about twelve hours beforehand will generally do the trick. A properly acclimated python will readily accept its food, offered either by its owner's hand or from the clutches of a long pair of forceps. Don't be surprised if it constricts a pre-killed mouse. Old habits die hard.

Feeding live mice to a ball python can prove dangerous to the snake, which may be injured by its prey. Frozen food is safer. *Michael A. Siino*

If you insist on feeding the snake live prey, feed in a small enclosure and throw some mouse food in along with the mouse to prevent the potentially hungry prey from attacking the resident predator. Feed with respect for both the mouse and the snake. This is not a neighborhood spectacle.

You must also monitor the process. Left unattended the snake may be injured, so if it's not hungry or if it is ill, it may not defend itself against a mouse attack. In the event of a lack of appetite, remove the mouse and try again later. A bad experience can stress the snake and lead to an anxiety-induced bout of fasting.

THE BALL PYTHON'S HOME

With reptiles cropping up in more and more households, specially designed products are becoming more available for their keeping. The ball python may therefore be housed in one of the elaborate custom setups designed specifically for healthy and attractive snake displays, or in a more traditional glass-type setup. Regardless of style, the enclosure must be designed specifically for snake-keeping, not for fish or hamsters.

Of primary concern is security. Whether the enclosure is made of glass, plexiglass, fiberglass or wood, it requires a door that provides good ventilation and that can be securely locked to prevent the consummate escape artist that is the ball python from doing so. Lockable sliding screen or plexiglass doors located either on the side or the top of the enclosure offer easy access as well as security, keeping the snake in and dogs, cats or other would-be predators out. Some enclosures boast more traditional hinge-type doors, but you must be able to keep these securely locked whenever the snake is at home.

Ideally, the enclosure should be as large as possible. Although a twenty-gallon tank size is usually considered the minimum acceptable for most adult ball pythons, larger being better, you may want to increase the size to something equivalent to a thirty-gallon or larger tank.

We cannot re-create the savannas of Africa within our living rooms, but we can make the ball python's home as healthy and comfortable as possible. This includes carpeting the enclosure with an appropriate snake-safe flooring material.

Layers of newspaper provide excellent, easily maintained flooring, for the layers can and should be removed on those rare occasions when the snake defecates or when the flooring becomes similarly soiled. More attractive to the eye are wood shavings, such as aspen shavings, or bark products, such as orchid or cypress bark. Steer clear of anything cedar or, for the most part, even pine, both of which can be heavy with oils dangerous to the snake. Avoid gravel, sand, or ground nut shells or corncobs, as well, for they may be swallowed by the snake and go on to cause digestive trouble.

No ball python wants a bare, empty enclosure to come home to, so furnish it with a large ceramic bowl of water. The bowl should be heavy enough not to tip over and large enough for the snake to soak in should it feel so

The proper ball python habitat includes a hiding place into which the snake may retreat for moments of privacy. *Michael A. Siino*

inclined, perhaps as a prelude to shedding, as a rest period following a meal or simply in response to high air temperatures. Change the water regularly, preferably every day (although don't disturb a soaking snake), and keep the dish clean.

Native to a region with vegetation and trees in which to hide, the ball python tends to value its privacy. Respect that natural instinct by providing it with a cardboard box, a tree-trunk-type log or a commercially available reptile cave in which it may retreat from curious eyes. Its hiding place should be large enough to hold and conceal the animal comfortably, with an opening that provides easy access.

You may also want to provide your pet with a branch for climbing, which, in a dual role, the snake can use as a rough surface to rub against when shedding begins. Like all furnishings in the enclosure, the branch must be free of parasites or any sharp edges that might cut the resident snake.

HEAT AND LIGHT AND THE BALL PYTHON

Ball pythons, being reptiles, are at the mercy of the external temperatures around them to provide them with adequate heating for their optimum body temperatures. Therefore they are at the mercy of their owners, whose responsibility it is to keep their homes properly heated and illuminated.

The temperatures within the python's enclosure must be in a gradient setup, in which the animal may move from one temperature to another. It should be able to find cooler temperatures on one end of the enclosure, warmer temperatures on the other. Ball pythons fare best in temperatures ranging from about 80 to 85 degrees Fahrenheit, although one end of the enclosure should be heated to about 90 to 95 degrees, where the snake can migrate should it feel the need to bask. At night, 75 degrees or so should suffice.

Providing that heat requires a commitment to detail and the right equipment. First, you must install at least two thermometers, the type that can attach to the outside of the enclosure for easy reading. These will help you maintain those ideal temperatures and prevent underheating and overheating, both of which can be deadly.

Heat may be provided via specially designed heating pads placed under the enclosure (they have been known to crack an enclosure's glass, so watch for relevant signs), incandescent lighting or ceramic heating elements. The ceramic products provide heat but no light, and are thus excellent nighttime heat sources for reptiles when installed at the top of one end of the enclosure.

Although they are frequently touted to the general public as necessary for reptiles, most reptile experts do not recommend the use of hot rocks. Too many reptiles have been burned by hot rocks run amok: The hot rock overheats, the reptile leans against it and sustains severe burns to the skin.

With such skin-to-hot-rock contact, snakes, and any basking reptile, can be severely injured by the time they realize something is amiss.

When arranging the habitat's heating elements, all must be situated so that the snake can move toward and away from the heat as its instincts see fit. By the same token, the snake must have ample room within the cage to escape from the higher heats. If possible, a system run by a thermostat will help to ensure that the heating elements do not overheat the enclosure, but for owners who cannot afford or accommodate such a system, more manual management will do the job, assuming the caretaker commits to routine monitoring of the elements to prevent overheating.

Some snake keepers use incandescent lighting positioned at one end of the enclosure as another type of heat source, although experts recommend that these be red incandescent lights to prevent overlighting. Some keepers also employ fluorescent full-spectrum lighting to facilitate nutrient assimilation during the day, although ball pythons are not typically pegged as a species that requires a great deal of light.

Although opinions vary somewhat over the ball python's lighting needs, all agree that the enclosure must be kept out of direct sunlight, which can over-heat both the enclosure and animal. Safety, too, must be paramount when designing the heating/lighting system. Observe basic electrical safety proto-cols, and remember that each system element is best positioned outside of the enclosure to prevent it from coming into direct contact with the snake. If an item must be set up inside, encase it in wire mesh to prevent potentially dangerous contact.

THE HEALTHY SNAKE

The ball python is a truly stunning creature that seems to have been created by a master sculptor working in gold, bronze and ebony. Sound attention to its health should help maintain that look, that healthy glow.

A healthy ball python appears alert and active. Its skin is clean, smooth and free of blisters, lesions or mites. The skin colors should be bright and vibrant. The healthy snake breathes smoothly and quietly, and, except at shedding time, its eyes are clear.

Unfortunately, that's about all you have to work with when evaluating your pet's health. Snakes usually show little or no sign of illness until the con-dition has progressed to a serious level. The following, however, will offer some basic guidelines on what the conscientious owner can look for.

Preventive Medicine. An important step toward keeping a ball python healthy is to locate a veterinarian who specializes in the care of reptiles long before you are in need of such a practitioner's services. Fortunately, this is not as difficult as it once was, as more veterinarians are mastering the care of these unique creatures.

Locating this expert early will prevent panic if you do notice signs of trouble. You never know when your pet may be in need of antibiotic therapy, parasite eradication or a special at-home treatment that the owner can learn to administer only from an experienced reptile veterinarian.

As for routine preventive health care, check the snake's breathing and eyes regularly; watch closely for any unusual changes in appearance or behavior, such as evidence of diarrhea; and evaluate calmly any loss of appetite that appears to undermine the snake's health, which will of course differ from a normal bout of fasting common to this species.

Run your hand down the snake's body periodically to check for any unusual skin or scale inconsistencies or lesions. The snake's body should feel relatively smooth and cool to the touch. Get to know how the snake feels when it is healthy, and you'll know right away when something changes.

External measures also contribute to a ball python's good health. Practice good hygiene within the snake's enclosure and maintain its temperature gradient at the appropriate levels. In addition, quarantine any new snake you bring home for sixty to ninety days. The newcomer should be housed in its own fully equipped enclosure, which should be kept in a separate room so as not to contaminate the existing animals.

Stress Prevention. As with all reptiles—and, frankly, all pets, whether they be warm and fuzzy or cool and scaly—do what you can to relieve and prevent stress in your pet ball python. It's no secret that stress can render the body ripe for illness in any living creature, whether it be snake or human, so don't frighten or overhandle the snake, and try not to handle it at inappropriate times.

Provide the python with a proper and clean environment with ample hiding places, and regulate its diet to prevent both obesity and malnutrition. Put yourself in the snake's skin and imagine what would be best for it and what it would like to see within its home. A sound management program, coupled with gentle, sensitive handling, will help prevent stress and thus the onset of stress-related health problems in the pet ball python.

A New Skin. Throughout its life, the ball python will shed its skin (the quickly growing young snake doing so more frequently than its elders). This is a vulnerable time for the snake. Several days before shedding, it will lose its appetite and possibly begin to rub up against rough surfaces. It may take a long soak in its water dish (make sure the water is clean), and its eyes may appear cloudy, its vision impaired. Feeding is off limits at this time, as is handling, for the vulnerable snake may be more inclined to bite.

A healthy snake will shed an intact skin. The skin over the eyes should shed as well. Shedding in patches may be read as a sign of possible illness or mite infestation, which will require veterinary attention.

Mouth Rot. When a snake, especially a weakened snake, injures its mouth, the result can be mouth rot, or stomatitis—and it can be fatal. This particular bacterial infection sets in, the mouth begins to rot, and, because the snake cannot eat, it will die.

The most graphic sign of mouth rot is the development of a furry, whitish, "cheesy-looking" growth on the tongue and around the mouth, which will, without treatment, ultimately spread and cover the entire mouth. As it spreads, the infection may ultimately gain access to the digestive tract.

Treatment of mouth rot must begin as soon as possible, for an affected snake will not eat, plus the condition can be highly contagious. Veterinary-conducted treatment consists of antibiotic therapy, usually administered directly to the infection site and perhaps by injection, as well. The veterinarian may also prescribe a care program that involves scrubbing the mouth and gums daily with a special solution formulated to combat this problem. Prevent the risk of mouth rot by keeping the snake healthy and well-nourished, protect it from injury and control potential stress inducers.

Parasites. Parasites may affect a snake both internally or externally. It's safe to assume that any wild-caught or even captive-hatched yet imported snake will be infected by both internal and external parasites, so get it to the veterinarian right away.

The owner may spot signs of internal parasites, perhaps roundworms or tapeworms that gained access to the snake's digestive tract through a mouse or rat the python had for dinner, in the snake's feces. These can be treated fairly easily by the vet.

External parasites, namely ticks and mites, will be visible on the skin. While the presence of ticks is fairly obvious, the ticks easily removed with alcohol and tweezers, mites present a more challenging, and potentially serious, problem. A mite infestation, usually evident in a snake's loss of appetite and shedding problems, should, like all parasites, be eradicated with the assistance of the veterinarian, for treatment involves the often long-term use of pesticides within the enclosure.

Respiratory Problems. A ball python subjected to temperatures lower than the ideal may be prone to respiratory problems. The obvious signs of such potentially fatal conditions include nasal congestion, evident in breathing difficulties and clogged nostrils, and a noticeable, health-diminishing loss of appetite. The snake may breathe through its mouth and hold its head back, staring up. Proper heat is a sound preventive agent, and an important aspect of treatment, which, again, should be pursued with the veterinarian's assistance.

The chinchilla, a native of the high Andes Mountains in South America and once a common resident of fur farms, has now found a more peaceful niche within the pet household. *Michael A. Siino*

CHAPTER 2

Rocky Mountain High: The Chinchilla

Once upon a time, chinchilla breeding was an immensely popular activity. It wasn't because chinchillas were cute, which they are. It wasn't because they are easy and interesting to care for, which they are. It was for a different reason entirely, and one not very pleasant for this unique and very fluffy little creature. Chinchillas were bred almost exclusively for their pelts.

A blessing. A curse. Both might define the lustrous signature coat of the chinchilla. Within the context of this animal's history, we might accurately say that the chinchilla was long ago blessed by nature with a coat designed perfectly for life in the rugged, rocky South American mountains from which it hails. It was also cursed by evolution with one of the thickest, softest, most luxurious coats in the animal kingdom.

Thanks to that curse, the chinchilla has for years been marked as a prime target by humans who craved a coat of that fur for their own, and by breeders (or ranchers as they are called) who sought to supply the necessary pelts to those covetous individuals.

In this day and age, the demand for fur of all kinds has decreased somewhat, boding well not only for chinchillas, but also for people looking for a quiet, fascinating companion animal with whom to share their homes.

Though the furrier's profits may be on the wane, the chinchilla breeder is still in business, breeding these incredibly soft, fluffy animals for a new niche: the pet household. It would thus be an understatement to say that the future is looking brighter all the time for the chinchilla.

The Chinchilla as a Pet

	Light	1	2	3	4	5	Heavy
TIME COMMITMENT				●			
MAINTENANCE Grooming					●		
Feeding				●			
General Clean-Up					●		
SUITABILITY TO CHILDREN Ages Infant-5	●						
Ages 5-10				●			
Over 10						●	
SOCIABILITY					●		
EXPENSE OF KEEPING				●			

WHAT IS A CHINCHILLA?

The chinchilla is a rodent, cousin to the rat, the mouse, the gerbil—he's the beautiful cousin of the family, you might say.

About the size of a guinea pig, the chinchilla has large, round ears; a bushy, squirrel-like tail; large button eyes; long whiskers; and a compact body made to look even more so by that coat of dense, usually grayish, fur, that covers it from head to toe.

But despite the image of the cuddly, squeezable stuffed toy it presents, the chinchilla is actually an example of evolution's finest work.

The Chinchilla's Origins

We think of chinchillas in conjunction with penthouses, champagne, caviar and limousines. But such terms have no place in the real story of the chinchilla, an animal that has been sculpted by life in one of the most remote, most treacherous, most barren regions on earth: the high Andes Mountains of South America.

Forced to survive in an area where Mother Nature exerts a great deal of pressure on her creations, the chinchilla has adapted perfectly to a life where water is scarce, the air and land are unfathomably dry, and the temperatures plunge regularly to frigid levels. To say this land is harsh can hardly describe what has molded the chinchilla into the animal we know today.

More than just a ball of fluff in appearance and behavior, each of the chinchilla's trademark characteristics has evolved for serious survival purposes. Its nocturnal nature is an adaptation that has protected it from predators, leading it instinctively to hide during daylight hours in the nooks and crannies of the rocks and caves that comprise its native landscape. Those large ears are evidence of an acute sense of hearing, while the large, round, dark eyes facilitate a clear sense of sight to help the creature both navigate those rocky cliffs and find food during its most active hours at dawn and dusk.

And then there is that coat, the most magnificent adaptation of all. Even when temperatures were their most frigid and conditions treacherous, the chinchilla in the wild could survive because of that almost supernaturally dense coat of hair. At the same time, the hair would protect it from predatory birds that might try to swoop down upon what they saw as a potential meal and lift it into the air. Engineered to fall easily away from its roots at the slightest tug, this precious defense mechanism would trick the bird. The predator would dive down for the kill, only to find that all it had as reward for its efforts was a mouthful of soft gray hair!

The ideal chinchilla habitat is a two-story cage equipped with shelves, a large exercise wheel and a dust bath. *Michael A. Siino*

Although there are relatively few chinchillas left in the wild these days, the demand for chinchillas as pets (most, if not all, of which are now captive bred) has been good for the species. It has taken many out of the fur trade and placed them in an environment with people who still retain a natural love of chinchilla fur, but prefer it remain on the chinchilla. As the chinchilla satisfies these individuals' pet-owning desires, the owners must return the favor by providing their pets with proper care.

THE CHINCHILLA'S BASIC NEEDS

The safest way to pursue chinchilla ownership is by heeding natural history and applying tips gleaned from this fascinating, even mysterious rodent's lifestyle in the wild to its life in captivity. For example, the chinchilla's home territories are extremely dry and barren, forcing the animal to subsist on a relatively sparse vegetarian diet of berries, grasses, bark and roots. Feeding the captive chinchilla a rich diet so readily available in civilization won't do the animal any favors.

With a fur structure that so exquisitely insulates it from extreme cold in its homeland, the captive chinchilla must be housed in a space where the temperatures never get too warm. A maximum air temperature of 68 degrees Fahrenheit is ideal, especially when that air is free of excess moisture, to which this animal is also unaccustomed and physically intolerant.

Genetically programmed to protect their precious coats, chinchillas are obsessively clean animals typically marked by only a faint odor. They spend a great deal of their time grooming themselves. You may feel inclined to assist in this by combing the animal from time to time, but this is usually not necessary. The same is true of external parasite control, for the healthy chinchilla's coat is too thick for fleas, lice and the like to launch an infestation.

The best way in which an owner can help groom the chinchilla is by pouring, so to speak, the animal a dust bath once or twice a week. The wild chinchilla, raised in a dry environment, learned to clean its fur in volcanic ash, a practice you may help it mimic at home. But more on that later.

As is to be expected, chinchillas shed. They usually shed and regrow their coats once a year, thus leaving fine light hairs around the house. For many owners these soft remnants become calling cards that simply make the house feel more like home because they indicate that chinchillas have been about.

CHINCHILLAS ARE SOCIAL ANIMALS

Given their nocturnal habits, chinchillas make great latchkey pets because they can nap during the day when the house is quiet, then awaken at the return of their owners in the afternoon or evening, ready for some family togetherness. The chinchilla does value its role as a member of the family unit, for, as a very social animal, it thrives in family groups, whether they be families of chinchillas or families of humans.

This means owners must be willing to lavish this animal with daily attention, most conveniently offered in the mornings and evenings. Despite their quiet natures, chinchillas can prove to be demanding animals. It is not fair to keep one locked in its cage twenty-four hours a day, offering it a bit of attention only at mealtime or when it's time to change the cage bedding.

For owners who take the time to interact with their chinchilla, the reward is the company of a friendly little animal that is as fun to watch as it is to touch. Chinchilla owners often find that they can just sit for hours watching the chinchilla as it sits back on its haunches, nibbling on a treasured treat it holds delicately in its hands. For others, it is the chinchilla hopping kangaroo-style about the furniture that holds the greatest fascination. Still others may most value the times when a pet chinchilla becomes stressed or frightened (perhaps when guests arrive and fail to observe the chinchilla house rules of decorum) and needs the soothing of a tickle behind the ears or under the chin from a familiar family member. Any way you look at it, these are all moments that make chinchilla ownership a delight.

THAT UNIQUE CHINCHILLA FUR

The texture or softness of the chinchilla's coat simply defies description. So soft you barely feel it kiss your fingertips. So soft you swear it must be lighter than air. It's all in the engineering.

The chinchilla is presumed to have the thickest, densest coat of fur on earth. Such a distinction rests on a unique structure in which as many as sixty hairs sprout from a single hair follicle, ready to slip out from their precarious anchor at the slightest tug exerted by the beak of a bird of prey—or the hands of an inconsiderate owner.

The coat is found in various shades of gray, as well as blond, black, charcoal and beige. The hairs, which can grow as long as an inch in length, are often darker at the base, lighter in the middle, and darker again at the tips. A combination of lightweight and stiffer, heavier hairs work together in a unified system that allows the hair to stand straight off the skin and effectively insulate the animal from the elements.

But softness and density are not all that are unique about the chinchilla's coat. In their home in the high mountains of South America, chinchillas would periodically "bathe" in the fine volcanic dust found there. Some wise and probably ancient instinct told them that if they rolled in the stuff, saturating their hairs with it, and then shook it off vigorously, it would rid the coat of excess oils and dirt that impaired this intricate system's effectiveness as insulator and defense mechanism. The instincts obviously proved correct, and today pet chinchillas still hear the call for dust baths. Their residence may have changed, but the care requirements of those luxurious coats have not.

TAKING A DUST BATH

We will let Petie be our guide in our exploration of this unique ritual. Petie is a two-year-old chinchilla who has just completed a rigorous workout on the exercise wheel. How fortunate that his owner chooses this particular moment to place the dust bath in the cage.

Petie targets the bath. One leap and he is immersed in a cloud of soft, airy dust. In ecstasy, he wriggles and waggles and spins and rolls, sending puffs of dust up all around him. The bath accomplishes just what Petie instinctively had hoped: massages him, cleanses him and removes the excess oils from his luxurious coat.

As we can see, though Petie resides in a modern urban household, he may still revel in the joy of the dust bath. And what an unexpected delight to witness a scene that was once observable only on the highest peaks of the Andes: a small animal whirling at such tornado-like speed you can hardly even tell it is an animal.

Petie's owner obviously understands the rules of the game. He knows to provide Petie not with sand or dirt, but with a fine, soft dust that closely resembles what wild chinchillas would find in their homeland. Fortunately, this material is today readily available in pet supply stores. This commercially marketed chinchilla dust is clean and sanitary, and will not foster microorganisms or other parasitic contaminants that might exist in material you might collect yourself.

The dust bath container is another important element. This should be a smooth-edged box or bowl made of plastic, wood or metal, with walls high enough to somewhat contain the flying dust that results from a vigorous bath. The overriding requirement is that the box be heavy and structured so that it cannot be toppled over by the bathing chinchilla within. Fill the box with the appropriate dust material, and the chinchilla will take care of the rest.

Like Petie's owner, you are wise to place the dust bath in the cage only two or three times a week, perhaps in the morning following a vigorous night of activity. You are wiser still to place it on top of a towel or newspaper to ease post-bath cleanup, a process further facilitated by placing a towel over the cage during the act itself to catch the inevitable flying dust.

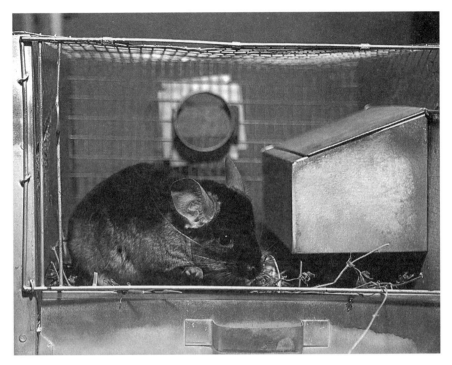

A chinchilla cage's built-in dust bath receptacle should have a closable top to prevent the chinchilla from soiling the soft ash-like dust within. *Michael A. Siino*

Remove the receptacle when bathtime is over to prevent the chinchilla from contaminating the dust by using the box as a litter box or a playpen. The dust is reusable. In regions where the air is more humid than a chinchilla is biologically accustomed to, more frequent baths may be necessary, but watch for signs of excessive scratching behavior, which could indicate that your chinchilla is overdoing it.

Thoroughly clean the "tub" and change the dust regularly—every two or three weeks—to keep it clean and free of germs. And stick to a bath schedule. Chinchillas are persnickety creatures and may adhere obsessively to a schedule. If they are denied their dust baths for an unusually long period of time, they may then refuse to take one again.

If your chinchilla goes on a permanent dust bath strike, a switch to water baths is *not* an option. Chinchillas and water don't mix, especially when the water has saturated their coats down to the skin. A traditional soap-and-water mode of bathing can remove the natural oils of the coat, strip it of its natural insulation properties and thus expose the chinchilla to illness.

SOCIALIZING WITH YOUR CHINCHILLA

The notion of living with one of, if not the, softest creatures on earth is indeed an attractive one. But you must work to earn the trust of this animal and agree to live by a few simple rules of conduct.

The rewards are worth the effort. Chinchillas tend to be calmer and exhibit more personality than do some of the other pet rodent species, such as hamsters and gerbils. Most chinchillas, though perhaps not demonstrably affectionate, are responsive, playful and easy to handle once they get to know their caretaker's scents and trust that their caretaker means them no harm.

Earning that trust means that you must acknowledge and respect the fact that chinchillas are naturally fearful of sudden movements and loud noises, either of which could invite a fear-induced bite. They require owners who are sensitive to this.

Chinchillas adapt well to cage life, as long as the cage is located in a quiet spot where they may remain unmolested during the day. Despite this adaptability, however, they do enjoy time outside their abodes, thriving on daily handling and social interaction with the humans in their lives.

Handling and Playing with Your Chinchilla

Once it gets to know you and becomes accustomed to your scent and touch, the chinchilla should feel secure sitting in your hands and enjoying a scratch behind the ears or under the chin. It may be trained to sit up and beg and even come when you call its name. Training sessions reap the greatest success when they are conducted with infinite patience and treat rewards. (Treats can also be an effective tool when it's time to lure a reluctant chinchilla back into its cage after a play session.) Many chinchillas have even been known to curl up and snooze on their owner's lap, a relaxing activity for both parties.

Indeed that type of quality time outside of the cage can be delightful for both chinchillas and their owners—as long as the chinchilla receives constant supervision, for its own safety and that of household furnishings. As a rodent with constantly growing teeth and an accompanying propensity to chew, the chinchilla may be inclined to chew virtually anything it finds in its path, be that a valuable wood carving, the new carpeting or a live electrical cord.

THE CHINCHILLA'S VOICE

The better you get to know the chinchilla, the more attuned you will become to its repertoire of sounds. These sounds range from bleats to purrs to whistling to the loud warning sounds it emits if it is frightened or startled. Avoid these by treating the chinchilla gently. In return, the chinchilla will probably get to know your sounds, too, so speak softly to the animal each day when you approach the cage and whenever you handle it. It will come to recognize your voice and rely on it as a soothing agent in times of stress.

MORE THAN ONE CHINCHILLA

If you do not have as much time as you would like to spend with your chinchilla, consider getting it a buddy—within limits, that is. Captive chinchillas can enjoy each other's company, but they can also become quite territorial, especially when the two chinchillas involved are males.

Chinchilla owners report no preference for a male or female; their characteristics are very similar. It's fairly easy to tell the difference between a male and a female, as the male's testicles are fairly visible.

Instead of housing a pair together, keep each in its own cage and place the cages next to each other. Even if the two chinchillas seem amenable to a closer partnership, it is usually wisest to keep them in separate quarters. With their cages side by side, they can bask in each other's company without having to share territory and possibly injuring each other in a duel.

As for relying on a different animal species as the chinchilla's companion, rethink that option. Opinions vary dramatically on the intelligence—and safety—of introducing chinchillas to other animals. You never know when a sudden look at a chinchilla will trigger a predatory response in a pet dog or cat. Then again, a dog or cat might seek fast friendship with this odd, fluffy creature.

Differing opinions converge, however, when those other animals you consider introducing to the chinchilla happen to be snakes and ferrets, mortal enemies of the chinchilla.

FINDING THE CHINCHILLA FOR YOU

With proper care and handling, a chinchilla should live an average of eight to ten years, but members of the species have been known to live even longer with optimum care. Even at the lower end of the average age range, they live much longer than most other rodent pet species. The moral of the story is that chinchilla ownership is a long-term commitment, a commitment that begins with choosing a healthy chinchilla pet with the potential to live up to its legacy.

A young chinchilla, a truly adorable critter, can leave its mother sometime between six to eight weeks of age. When confronted with a passel of these wonderful creatures either at a pet shop or at a breeder's facility, try to keep your mind on the task at hand: choosing a healthy, friendly pet that has been raised and socialized in a clean, hygienic, low-stress environment.

Health will glow most warmly from the chinchilla that has bright, twinkling eyes and a clean, fluffy, lustrous-looking coat that is free from signs of hair loss or chewed fur. Healthy ears will also appear clean, and the animal shouldn't mind being handled very gently. Avoid chinchillas with watery eyes, a runny nose or an unkempt coat, the latter of which could indicate temperament problems or malnutrition.

Like all rodents, the chinchilla's teeth will continue to grow throughout its lifetime. The animal's long-term health and contentment, therefore, rely on the continued health and proper structure of the teeth and jaws. Although a very young chinchilla's teeth will be white, those pearly whites will turn to pearly oranges (yes, orange) or orange-yellows as the animal matures. Steer clear of the animal that seems to be drooling; this could be a sign of tooth problems or a genetic deformity of the jaw.

Temperament, too, should be a key target in your evaluation. You will want to handle your prospective pet, but in doing so remember that these are gentle, sensitive, quiet animals that prefer owners with similar qualities. Mind your best manners when introducing yourself to a chinchilla. Approach the animal's cage quietly. If it at first backs away, be patient. If, on the other hand, its immediate reaction is to bite, that could be a sign that the breeder didn't take the time to socialize the animal during its formative weeks.

If you go looking for your pet during the daytime (which most of us do), remember that you will be meeting this animal during the middle of its night. Don't worry if it doesn't seem quite as active and energetic as you expected.

You may buy chinchillas most readily from pet shops, and assuming a specimen looks healthy, you are probably safe in doing so. Breeders are another good source if there is one in your area, but again, these may be few and far between. To date, there are no organizations devoted to chinchillas, so you should ask veterinarians or pet shop owners for advice on where to find this pet.

NIBBLING AND LIFTING

You do want a chinchilla that is amenable to handling, so introduce it to this concept with gradual, deliberate motion. Slowly place your hand at the door of the cage, or, if the chinchilla seems willing and interested, in the cage. Allow it to come forward and sniff your hand. Don't be alarmed if the chinchilla then begins to gently nibble your fingertips, your sleeve, your rings, your watch—anything it deems it must to get to know you. Chinchillas nibble to trim their teeth, but they also do it to show affection and to investigate their surroundings. If you are the recipient of such nibbles, you may view this as a high compliment and an invitation to pick the animal up.

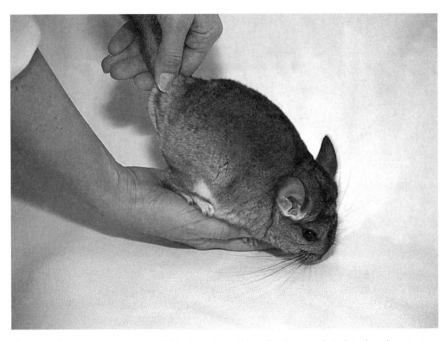

To lift a chinchilla, grasp its tail firmly yet gently at the base. Lift its hind end up just enough so you can scoop your other hand under the animal's body and give it full support as you raise it aloft. *Michael A. Siino*

Because of its tender skin and the ease in which hairs will slip from their follicles, you can pick up a chinchilla by gently grasping the animal by the base of the tail with one hand, and then lifting the back side of its body slightly up off the surface it stands on. This gives you the opportunity to then scoop your other hand underneath the chinchilla's body for full support during lifting and holding. Some owners vehemently oppose the idea of lifting the chinchilla by the tail, but that really isn't what you are doing with this method. Far from dangling the animal in the air by its tail, with this method you are providing it with overall support and protecting the coat at the same time.

BRINGING YOUR CHINCHILLA HOME

So, you have conducted an in-depth evaluation, chosen a delightful chinchilla companion and you are transporting it to its new home. This is no time to drop the good manners. Once you bring a chinchilla home, you must maintain that dignified demeanor.

You must never frighten this animal, which may be easily stressed. Fright will manifest itself in the screams and cries of the affected chinchilla. On the flip side, when content, the animal may chatter and chirp in appreciation of your gentle handling, leaving you to feel most honored to be the recipient of such conversation.

Housing Your Chinchilla

The basics of chinchilla housing are just that: basic. The chinchilla needs a clean roomy cage with a door that locks securely. This must of course be made of gnaw-proof, rust-proof material. If you are truly seeking your pet's infinite devotion, choose a two-story vertical cage setup instead of a typical rodent cage. This airy design, complete with shelf-like platforms positioned at various heights, feeds this mountain dweller's desire to climb and move about. It also provides the animal with ample opportunity to run and jump and get lots of exercise when it is up and about at night while its family is trying to sleep.

Inside the cage the chinchilla needs separate areas for separate functions. The animal must have a hiding box, something like a small cardboard box with a hole cut in one side for a door. This hiding box will do dual duty as a bed, a critical amenity for this nocturnal creature that will spend a good part of the day sleeping. The chinchilla will probably gnaw on the cardboard box, but simply replacing it occasionally will solve that problem. Soft plastic, another option, can be dangerous to an active chewer, so it's best to stick with a cardboard box.

Chinchillas need and like to play when they're awake. The play area should contain a collection of favored toys, perhaps an exercise wheel, a hardwood block and/or an untreated fruit tree branch for chewing, and a four-inch-wide chew-resistant pipe segment for play and hiding.

There should be an eating area with a heavy, ceramic food dish. Chinchillas need to chew on hay, so hang a hay rack to the side of the cage to keep the hay clean and dry. The cage wall will also host the chinchilla's water source: A clean water bottle designed for rodents with a metal spout that can't be chewed.

If the floor of the cage is solid, which is preferred because this is easier on the animal's feet, cover that floor with two or three inches of bedding material. This may be pine shavings (only those without resins or other chemical treatments), aspen shavings or newspaper-based products available at pet supply stores. Avoid cedar shavings, which can cause respiratory or skin troubles.

Cleaning Up After the Chinchilla

The only unpleasant aromatic aspect to chinchilla-keeping tends to be the odor of their urine in their habitat. You can keep this in check by, first, installing a litter pan filled with non-clumping cat litter or bedding material in the area the animal designates as its bathroom. Second, remove soiled bedding from the cage daily to prevent dampness or fungal growth. Replace all the bedding on a weekly or biweekly basis as needed and clean and disinfect the structure of the cage every few weeks.

Where to Put Your Chinchilla's House

Where most chinchilla keepers make their major mistakes is not in the basic housing structure and amenities, but rather in cage atmosphere and position.

Even the most well-appointed chinchilla habitat can spawn stress in its occupant if it is located in a noisy, high-traffic area of the owner's home. Cage placement has everything to do with this nocturnal being's sleeping schedule. The animal should be put in a quiet spot, a place that will likewise benefit the human family members during the night when they are sleeping

As nocturnal creatures, chinchillas should be afforded peace and quiet during the day in keeping with their natural biological rhythms. *Michael A. Siino*

and the chinchilla is at play—chewing, jumping, perhaps chirping. In other words, position the cage where the family won't disturb the chinchilla during the day, and the chinchilla won't disturb the family at night.

Light is another issue. Chinchillas don't care for bright lights, as these, like noise, make sleep rather difficult. In addition to the hiding box for daytime slumber, some owners cover at least half the cage with a sheet or towel during the daytime hours to provide even more privacy.

Light, Heat and Humidity

Direct sunlight should be avoided because of its disruptive effects on sleep and because chinchillas are most active in cooler temperatures. Chinchillas should fare well in a home maintained at below 75 degrees Fahrenheit (preferably lower), so don't be surprised if your air conditioning bills increase during the summer solely for the sake of your chinchilla.

Humidity presents an even greater threat than does heat to this animal. Far too often, owners inadvertently house chinchillas in too humid of an environment, perhaps ignorant of the fact that these animals have no tolerance for humidity and must be kept in dry, cool, well-ventilated surroundings. A damp garage or basement, a rainy backyard or any moist place is not suitable as an appropriate site for a chinchilla's cage.

This young chinchilla feeds on some loose alfalfa hay. Chinchillas are creatures of habit and like to eat at regular times each day. *Michael A. Siino*

FEEDING THE CHINCHILLA

Feeding chinchillas is a relatively simple process. A high-quality pelleted chinchilla feed or chow, formulated specifically for this vegetarian species, is available from several manufacturers. This should comprise the bulk of the diet (in the absence of chinchilla pellets, rabbit feed is a good substitute). Supplement this with clean dry hay, alfalfa or timothy hay, loose or pelleted. While the chinchilla feed satisfies the animal's basic nutritional needs, the hay provides the necessary roughage.

Creatures of habit that they are, chinchillas should be fed at regular times each day. Chinchillas learn quickly to tell time and know when the dinner bell is late. There is some instinctive method to this madness, for, given the animals' evolutionary background, chinchilla digestive tracts seem to operate best when the food is simple and fed in moderate amounts. Serving dinner at the same times each day can actually prevent gastric upset.

As a guideline, feed the chinchilla once in the morning and once in the evening. Each meal should consist of a tablespoon of pellets and, once a day, a handful of hay. The diet must be further supplemented by clean water that should always be available in the cage water bottle. Make sure the feed and water are fresh to avoid diarrhea, and you're in business. It's that simple.

To embellish the process—and the menu—is to invite unnecessary trouble. Excess feed, for example, can lead to digestive upset and constipation in the chinchilla, as can an overdose of treats. This does not mean that chinchillas should not be offered treats. Treats must be fed in moderation and should only be treats that are healthy for chinchillas.

Chinchilla Treats

Chosen by chinchillas themselves as some of the all-time favorite chinchilla treats are raisins, raw oatmeal flakes and apple slices. When offered one of these culinary treasures (not too frequently, of course), the chinchilla will hold the morsel in its small front paws and nibble happily, presenting a picture so delightful, you may feel inclined to offer more just to be able to see the scene continue. You must, however, resist. Take a picture instead.

MAINTAINING GOOD HEALTH

You owe it to the potentially long-lived chinchilla to provide it with the best care possible, an eye always on the maintenance of good health and contentment. Continued health depends first on an owner who is attuned to the signs of potential problems, and second, on that same owner's commitment to a program of preventive care.

Check your chinchilla for signs of good health: bright, clear eyes, healthy skin and coat, good appetite and activity level. *Michael A. Siino*

Finding a veterinarian for a chinchilla is easier now than it once was, because more and more vets are specializing in the more unusual pet species. Shopping around (and getting references) and querying other chinchilla owners is the best way to go. The key is that you definitely want someone who is experienced with chinchillas, which is what word-of-mouth recommendations will indicate. In doing such research, ask the references as well as the practitioner about his or her experience with and knowledge about such issues as tooth care, longevity and rodent diseases. Even ask questions to which you already know the answers; for example, if the prospective vet suggests using sand in the dust bath, look for another vet.

It may also help to ask owners of other rodent species and of rabbits, as they probably know of good practitioners in the area. One convenient place to do this is at state and county fairs, where exhibitors and breeders congregate and are usually thrilled to share their expertise and recom-mendations on everything from dental care, to diet, to local veterinary services.

Warning signs that might indicate a problem include diarrhea or any change in feces consistency (droppings should normally be dry, dark and small), a loss of appetite, and listlessness or any other sudden change in behavior or attitude. A lack of droppings obviously indicates constipation, which is not all that unusual in chinchillas. This is another reason for feeding these animals on time, and, further, for avoiding any changes in diet components or helping amounts.

Look for signs of health—good or ill—in the chinchilla's hair and skin, as well. Aside from being indicators of internal problems and malnutrition that might show in a dull coat or hair loss, the hair and skin themselves can be affected by problems. For instance, if you notice a scaliness on the animal's skin or even a dandruffy residue, particularly on the ears, feet and/or nose, your chinchilla could be suffering from a skin fungus. This is a common development when the hygiene within the chinchilla's habitat is not up to the animal's high standards of excellence.

If you notice that your pet's fur appears dark, uneven and unkempt, the animal may be engaging in fur eating. While this is common among chinchillas housed together, it can crop up in the solitary chinchilla who is nervous and stressed. Consider these factors: Perhaps it has no privacy within its cage. Perhaps the environment is noisy and frightening to this sensitive creature. Maybe the air is too warm or too humid. Is the chinchilla's diet of poor quality? Have you made any sudden changes in feeding times or feed brand? All of these can lead to fur chewing, and all, of course, are easily corrected by reversing the problem.

Finding a Competent Veterinarian

If you do suspect a problem, the quicker you seek treatment for the animal, the better. Fortunately, it is not as difficult as it might seem to find a veterinarian skilled in treating chinchillas. This is due in part to the fact that the more unusual pet species are attracting owners who are willing to take them to the veterinarian, and veterinary specialties are reflecting that trend. Chinchillas have further benefited because of their traditional role in the fur trade. Though unfortunate for the animals, the fur trade provided motivation for researchers to pay attention to chinchillas' health and care.

Meanwhile, back at the ranch, so to speak, commit to hygienic care practices. Clean and disinfect the chinchilla's habitat regularly. Remove uneaten food, soiled bedding and feces daily. Wash the food dish at each feeding time, and clean the water bottle while you're at it.

At the same time, use the proper supplies required for optimum chinchilla care. Fill the dust bath with the correct type of fine, absorbent dust, use the right clippers when it's time to trim the chinchilla's toenails, and feed only the freshest food. Don't skimp or look for shortcuts. To do so is to endanger the health of one of petdom's most fascinating creatures.

Although it is frequently and mistakenly referred to as a wild animal, the ferret has been domesticated for thousands of years. *Michael A. Siino*

CHAPTER 3

Born to Play: The Ferret

A female ferret goes into heat. A few weeks later she dies, her well-meaning owner learning too late that if an intact female is not bred during her heat cycle, she will not survive.

A doting parent places the family's pet ferret in the crib with a crying baby, hoping the soft, warm "toy" will bring an end to the youngster's howls. Terrified and trapped, the ferret bites the child.

Mistaking the tunnel-shaped lump in the living room rug for just that—a tunnel-shaped lump in the living room rug—an absent-minded ferret owner seriously injures his pet when he steps down on what the animal chose as a cozy hiding place.

Each of these stories is true. The scenes they depict have in fact occurred time and time again in ferret-owning households all across the country. They illustrate clearly the fact not that ferrets are accident-prone, vicious little creatures, but that few pet species are as plagued by tales of irresponsible ownership as is the sprightly ferret.

Yet each of these events could also have been prevented and therein lies their silver lining. In heeding the particulars of these stories, prospective ferret owners are offered the opportunity to carry their messages forward to ensure that future ferrets are cared for properly and understood and appreciated for the unique little animals that they are.

WHAT IS A FERRET?

A mean little critter with a temper and a very bad odor? To many, this is the description of the ferret. There is in fact some truth to that image, but placed in a realistic context, this picture is not all that it would seem.

The Ferret as a Pet

	Light	1	2	3	4	5	Heavy
TIME COMMITMENT						✦	
MAINTENANCE Grooming						✦	
Feeding				✦			
General Clean-Up					✦		
SUITABILITY TO CHILDREN Ages Infant-5	✦						
Ages 5-10			✦				
Over 10					✦		
SOCIABILITY						✦	
EXPENSE OF KEEPING					✦		

The domestic ferret is a member of the rather odoriferous *Mustelidae* family, cousin to the skunk, the mink, the weasel, the otter and the badger. Not to be confused with the black-footed ferret, a wild and endangered species, the domestic ferret has been sharing human domiciles for thousands of years, probably even longer than has the cat. Coveted by humans for its skills in rodent hunting, it was long recruited for that job in Egypt and Europe, and ultimately in the United States, as well.

Despite its history, today the ferret is a controversial pet species whose place in American homes is frequently debated in both private and public arenas. Indeed no one pet species is ideal for every owner or family, and the ferret is no exception.

In appearance, the ferret resembles a long, wiry sock puppet with a small head; an animated, often irresistible expression; a slim, tubular physique; and short legs that carry it with lightning speed across the ground. Its flexibility and willowy movements may lead some to believe that the ferret's body cannot possibly contain a skeleton, a suspicion bolstered by its skills as escape artist extraordinaire.

Ferrets generally grow to weigh between two and five pounds, males typically growing larger than females. The healthy, properly cared for ferret has clear eyes; long whiskers (with which to explore its world); a soft, shimmery

The ferret resembles a long, wiry sock puppet with a small head and animated expression. *Michael A. Siino*

coat that may be a variety of attractive colors; a clean genital area and an insatiably curious, affectionate nature. A healthy start as a youngster, along with an owner's conscientious commitment to its long-term care, can help the little animal live to a ripe old age of eight to eleven years.

But what about that image of the ferret as vicious and pungent and an all-around inappropriate pet? Well, on the pet spectrum, ferrets stand somewhere between the dog and the cat. They are less dependent on humans than is the dog, but more dependent than the cat. They are passionately interested, almost obsessively so, in their family's activities, another very dog-like characteristic. But beyond such comparisons, they possess their own unique language and their own unique impression of the world.

Ferrets do bite, primarily in play, and a ferret bite feels similar to that of a puppy's sharp-toothed nips. They will also bite out of fear, and quite effectively, especially when they are being held too tightly or by someone they do not trust. They are therefore considered more appropriate pets for adults than for children, and should be kept clear of infants altogether.

FERRETS AND CHILDREN

Such groups as the American Medical Association and the American Veterinary Medical Association have conducted studies of cases in which ferrets have attacked children, the results invariably indicating that had the parents been more responsible in handling the ferrets and managing the children, the events would not have occurred.

In a typical scene, the ferret is attracted to those irresistible scents that tend to linger around the mouth of a child, placing both in a rather precarious situation that promises to ignite the moment the youngster attempts to squeeze or pull the tail of the soft sock toy sniffing around its face. The conclusion remains clear. Ferrets and small children do not mix and should be kept apart, for the safety of both the child and the ferret.

FERRET BEHAVIOR

Ferrets will not tolerate rough handling. They thrive best in the care of owners who respect this and are willing to explore the nuances of ferret language. Both will enhance the relationship that can build between ferret and human.

As those who have taken the time to explore the world of the ferret can attest, ferrets will run backwards when they are feeling anxious or unsure. As the intuitive owner understands, they will often lunge forward in a manner that suggests aggression, but that is actually an act of play. When frightened or injured they will scream, they will hiss when they are afraid, and they will cluck when either happy or angry (leaving the owner to translate which is being expressed at a given moment according to the context in which the sound is made).

FERRET TRAINING

Because of their naturally curious, fun-loving natures, some ferrets can be trained to walk willingly on a leash, and most will learn to sit on their owner's shoulder and obey simple commands, including the word "no," which, as any ferret owner can testify, can be an infinitely handy tool.

Obsessively clean creatures, ferrets can also learn to use a litter box. They must, however, be introduced to all such concepts with gentle patience, positive reinforcements (i.e., treat rewards) and consistency. Aggressive, domineering handling has no place in the responsible care of ferrets.

STINKY CRITTERS

While ferrets demand cleanliness in both themselves and their surroundings, they are by no means odor-free. Quite the opposite. One characteristic they share with others in their family is the presence of anal scent glands that produce a musky odor that few humans find pleasant. These glands can be

Most ferrets enjoy hitching
a ride on a trusted owner's
shoulder, but they need to
be trained to do so.
Michael A. Siino

removed surgically when the ferret is very young, but even if they are, some odor will remain.

The ferret's odor, which is usually more pronounced in males than in females, kicks in when the animal reaches about six months of age. Needless to say, this will come as a surprise to an owner who was not apprised of this inevitability by an unscrupulous breeder or ferret seller. Thus, taking the time to learn about all the unique characteristics that can make living with ferrets such a challenge, albeit a joyful one for the right owner, is the greatest favor one can do for his or her new pet.

ILLEGAL IN SOME STATES

Before bringing a ferret into the home, a prospective owner should first find out if he or she is legally allowed to keep a ferret. Amid emotional charges of viciousness of loose ferrets on flocks of domestic poultry, herds of undefined livestock animals and agricultural crops, ferrets are not necessarily welcomed in every community. Laws have in turn been passed to prevent their ownership and to mandate confiscation of these ferrets if kept illegally.

Yet even though some people and some communities have labeled ferrets inappropriate as pets, the fact remains that their popularity has increased dramatically in the past decade, even within the states that have deemed ferret-keeping illegal. If people are going to live with ferrets, legally or otherwise, it is only fair that they understand what they are up against and commit responsibly to their pets' care.

Upon publication of this book, California and Hawaii will be the only remaining states where ferrets remain illegal. California enthusiasts have been trying periodically to push a law through that will end the ferret's illegal status in their state, and eventually they will succeed, but there are no plans to follow suit in Hawaii. There are many ferrets who live quite happily, though secretively, with their California owners.

YOUR FERRET'S HEALTH

As with any pet species, ferrets require a unique care curriculum. In addition, the owners of these animals must deal with broader external issues that rarely affect more common pet species. For instance, sound veterinary care is critical to a ferret's long-term health, yet it can be tricky finding a practitioner skilled in ferret care—especially in those areas that outlaw ferret ownership.

Finding a good ferret veterinarian is not much different from finding a good vet for a dog or a cat. Other ferret owners are the best sources for information on skilled, ferret-friendly vets in the area, as are staff members at animal shelters and ferret rescue groups. Even other veterinarians who don't treat ferrets probably know who among their colleagues do offer such services. In California, where veterinarians cannot necessarily advertise their treatment of ferrets, owners can consult such groups as the California Domestic Ferret Association and Ferrets Anonymous (listed in Appendix).

The fledgling ferret owner should understand that the ferret's required veterinary regimen begins when the animal is quite young, ideally between six and eight weeks of age. This, say experts, is not only the minimum age at which a young ferret should be introduced to its new home, but also the ideal time to have the young ferret spayed or neutered and descented (the two procedures can and should be done at the same time).

There are those among the ferret-owning community who condemn the practice of descenting, deeming it cruel and unnecessary. They promote weekly baths to keep the ferret sweet-smelling as an alternative. While that position is commendable and understandable, in today's climate descenting might give the ferret even more of a chance at remaining within its home for the long haul.

While descenting may be optional, there is no question that the pet ferret should be spayed or neutered. Neutering will help ease a male's aggressive tendencies, and spaying will literally save a female's life. Once the female enters her heat cycle, she must be bred or she can die of a condition known as aplastic anemia. Spaying removes that risk and prevents cancers associated with the reproductive organs in the female.

Neutering does the same for the male, with the secondary benefit of mellowing his temperament into one more acceptable to the prospective pet household. The neutered male will probably be more interested in his owner than in other ferrets, and he may exhibit no interest in partaking of the irritating habit of scent marking the home.

SIGNS OF A SICK FERRET

While altering does foster health, even an altered ferret is not immune from potential illness. The classic signs of an ill ferret include a loss of appetite, a dull haircoat, diarrhea (especially if tinged with blood), unclean ears, listless behavior and watery eyes. These signs are difficult to miss in so lively an animal as the ferret. Establish a relationship ahead of time with a veterinarian skilled in treating ferrets before treatment is needed. You should also get to know your pet ferret well so you'll notice immediately if anything is amiss.

Ferrets are highly susceptible to the common cold, which they can contract from their owners and from other ferrets. They may also fall victim to pneumonia, feline and canine distemper and rabies. As canine distemper is a particularly dangerous threat, ferrets must be vaccinated against the disease. The young ferret should receive its first distemper vaccines in a series at six, ten and fourteen weeks of age, followed by a booster every year thereafter. If you are at all uncertain about whether a new pet ferret has been vaccinated against canine distemper, have it done immediately.

In 1990, the U.S. Department of Agriculture approved a rabies vaccine for ferrets, momentarily quieting opponents of ferret ownership who had long cited the lack of a vaccine as a reason the animals should remain illegal as pets. But because so little is known about the manifestation of the disease in this species, some public health policies may still mandate that a vaccinated ferret be destroyed in the event of a bite incident. Nevertheless, the vaccine is important in the protection it offers the ferret, as well as the peace of mind it can offer a ferret owner (and the ferret owner's ferretphobic guests).

IRRESISTIBLE, AND YET . . .

Many among us are just naturally attracted to ferrets. We can't help it. One look at that wiggling nose, the soft sleek physique and those bright eyes that are the products of a sharp mind and a terminally adventurous spirit, and we are forever this animal's hostage. We humans as a species tend to gravitate naturally toward those who like us. We thus find the ferret's unabashed affinity for us, and for everything we do, to be absolutely irresistible.

But despite how flattering we may find these complimentary ferret sentiments, we must not react to them casually or impulsively by using them alone as our reasons for taking a ferret as a pet. As demanding an animal as it is, possessed of that sharp mind and adventurous spirit that holds us so enraptured, the ferret in turn requires a mellow, relaxed owner whose greatest attribute is his or her sense of humor. Only then can you successfully coexist with the ferret.

Once you have honestly evaluated your sense of humor, your sense of responsibility and your sense of, shall we say, self-sacrifice, and deemed them up to the challenge of ferret care, you may begin the search for a pet that promises to throw your entire home into happy disarray.

FINDING THE FERRET FOR YOU

The best pet prospect is a young, human-raised animal (some find females the easiest to live with), or an older ferret with only positive experiences with humans. In addition to exhibiting fine physical characteristics and a lively demeanor, the animal should be comfortable with humans, willing to bond readily with them because of age and breeding. Ideally it should have already been spayed or neutered and descented.

A responsible breeder is the best source for such an animal, as he or she plays a key role in ensuring the animal will enjoy a long and healthy life. A good ferret breeder pays attention to his or her animals' temperament and health as well as to their physical appearance. A good breeder also takes great care to ensure that the new owner understands the challenges of ferret care, doing everything possible to prevent future problems that will throw a wrench in what can and should be a long and rewarding relationship. Such a breeder is usually best located through word-of-mouth from other satisfied ferret owners, through local ferret clubs or through referrals from veterinarians who specialize in unusual and exotic pets.

Some experienced ferret keepers believe that a particular ferret's propensity to attack or to otherwise behave with extreme aggression may have something to do with family lines. Heed this message, and work only with those breeders who emphasize temperament, temperament, temperament.

It is not difficult to recognize such an individual. When speaking with a breeder of this sort, you will find that such words as "socialization" and "neutering" take precedence over words like "cute" and "color." You will no doubt find evidence in the animals this individual breeds, as well. There is a dramatic difference between a healthy, well-bred, well-socialized, people-loving ferret who learned to live and play with humans at a very young age, and one that has been bred as a commodity.

The responsible breeder will also inquire into the ferret's prospective living situation and show concern if there are children in the family. Most

With its wiggling nose, bright eyes and curious nature, it's easy to see why so many come under the spell of this demanding pet. *Michael A. Siino*

responsible owners agree that these are not pets for children, especially small infants, who tend to be the victims of most ferret attacks. In most such cases, an adult is at fault for putting the ferret and child together in an enclosed area, or for otherwise forcing the ferret to interact with this frightening noisy creature with flailing, grabbing hands and a tendency to squeeze. The blame falls on the adult who has failed to respect the ferret's nature and ensure the child's safety. Respect for and supervision of a ferret are critical in any ferret household, with or without children.

A latch-key home, where the owners are away from the house most of the time, is also not appropriate for a pet of this type. This problem may be alleviated somewhat by keeping more than one ferret, thus providing the animals with playmates who can entertain each other while the human members of the family are away. But even then a ferret, or even a pair of ferrets, is better suited to people who are willing to put in the time and effort that these animals demand.

Male or Female?

Many a breeder and owner will proclaim that a spayed female is the ideal ferret pet—that males, even neutered males, tend to be more aggressive and carry a stronger odor. This author has been around many well-cared-for neutered males that were just as fun-loving and devoted to their owners as were females—and no stinkier.

The key is that the animals, male or female, come from conscientious breeders who make the effort to spay or neuter the animals they sell as well as socialize them at an early age so they're accustomed to other animals and people.

Although the testicles are noticeable on the male, it is still best to deal with a trusted breeder who can guarantee a prospective pet's gender, and the pet should be spayed or neutered before going to its new home.

FERRETS NEED AFFECTION

Ferrets require a great deal of attention and interaction. Even when they discover a game with which they can entertain themselves outside of their cage, they require constant supervision, just as a young toddler would. They can vanish instantly into the furniture, a kitchen cupboard, you name it.

Choose a ferret for a pet and you take on the responsibility of an animal you must follow around and supervise constantly, an animal that will handily dismantle your abode if you allow it to roam free while you are not at home,

Ferrets need constant supervision when out of their enclosures. They are escape artists and curious about everything. *Michael A. Siino*

an animal that will come to dominate the household—an animal that the right owner simply cannot imagine living without.

WHAT YOUR FERRET WILL NEED AT HOME

Let us imagine a prospective ferret owner who has done the necessary homework and made the decision that he cannot live without a ferret in the house. He chooses his new pet; say, a nine-week-old fawn-colored female who has been socialized, spayed and descented while in the care of her breeder. But before our new owner brings his little pet home, he must prepare for her arrival. She must have a home of her own within the home at large.

First, the cage. Ferrets cannot be given free run of the home without supervision, so they must have a safe, secure haven to call their own. A ferret will fare best in a large, sturdy metal cage with a solid floor to protect the animal's toes and a secure door latch that can withstand those extraordinary escaping skills. Also critical is that the cage be well-ventilated and roomy, a requirement many owners meet by building their own ferret living quarters out of a combination of wood or piping and wire, or by converting a large wooden hutch typically used for rabbits housed outdoors.

Ferrets themselves may be housed outdoors, but they should still be treated to daily visits indoors, as well, for they must feel as though they are a part of the family. If the ferret is kept outdoors, its cage, which also must be large, well-ventilated and secure, must be situated out of direct sunlight, drafts, precipitation, or extreme heat or cold. The floor of the cage should be carpeted with a bedding of clean hay, straw or wood shavings (cedar or sawdust can cause respiratory illness; aspen is preferable).

In keeping with the ferret's fastidious living habits, the cage must be large enough to be divided into three separate sections: one for sleeping, one for eating and one for eliminating. The latter area is where you should put the in-cage litter box.

Teach the animal to use the box by watching for the restlessness that usually precedes the need to eliminate. Place the ferret in the box and praise it profusely for doing its business. Don't bother correcting the animal if it doesn't make it to the box in time. That will do no good. Only positive reinforcement will get the message across.

Ferrets also need a place to hide within their cage. The bed can serve dual duty here. An enclosed box of cardboard or plastic with a clean, soft, cotton cloth, blanket or towel inside for bedding can sit in the corner of the cage and serve as both bed and hiding place for a fortunate ferret—especially an older ferret, which will require more sleep than will its younger counterpart.

Because ferrets are basically nocturnal, and are thus more active at night than they are during the middle of the day, the enclosed sleeping/hiding box can provide sanctuary to a ferret attempting to escape the light of day and rest up for the wonderful activities that await in the late afternoon and evening.

From that first day forward the cage must be kept as clean as possible. Demanding cleanliness in both itself and its home, the ferret will do what it can to meet this goal, but it will require some housekeeping assistance from its owner to ensure that feces are removed regularly, bedding remains clean and dry, and uneaten food, which the ferret may be inclined to hide in her bed (or in her owner's bed), is removed before it spoils. If the cage is not sufficiently cleaned and well-situated, its occupant may become neurotic and even grow ill.

In addition to the sleeping box and the litter box filled with clean cat litter, other critical ferret amenities include a heavy food dish that can withstand a ferret's playful attempts to overturn it and a clean spout-style water bottle filled daily with fresh water. The fact that most ferrets enjoy splashing around in water presented to them in a dish explains why a water bottle is the superior water receptacle.

It's wise to provide the ferret with some of these staple accoutrements outside of the cage as well, such as a food dish and water bottle in the kitchen, and a litter box in every room in which the ferret may roam. Those extra

The well-designed ferret abode has separate areas for a sleeping box, food and water and the litter box. It is also escape-proof. *Michael A. Siino*

litter boxes are especially handy; the ferret will find one always available when the urge strikes, which is typically after a nap or a meal.

Letting Your Ferret Settle In

When the young ferret first arrives at its new home, it should be afforded several quiet days to get accustomed to its cage and the new people, scents and sights in its life. As the ferret comes to feel more secure and trusting, its playful, affectionate ferret nature will begin to emerge, setting the stage for short play and handling sessions with its new owner.

Before the ferret is allowed to begin exploring the home at large, the owner is wise to do some ferret-proofing of that part of the ferret's soon-to-be environment. Potentially dangerous temptations, such as holes in a wall or screen door that might invite the attention of a ferret seeking a hiding place or escape outlet, should be tended to immediately, as should such everyday ferret temptations as open windows or exposed electrical wires.

Such safety checks must occur every time the ferret is given free yet supervised run of the house: before, during and after. Safety patrol should become a routine part of the management of a household in which a ferret resides.

With a ferret in the house everyone must be on constant safety watch. In time it will become second nature to all to remain ever on the lookout for such potential dangers as open doors, windows and ovens; to take uncommon care in negotiating around the tubular-shaped lump in the living room rug; and to refrain from sitting in the recliner in the family room, which, to be honest, should be disposed of as soon as possible. According to the California Domestic Ferret Association, these chairs are a leading cause of death in young ferrets and have absolutely no redeeming value as far as ferret safety is concerned.

FERRETS, FAMILY AND OTHER PETS

Basking in the patience and care it reaps from its owner, the ferret will soon learn to develop its own routine within the household. It may even learn to get along with other pets (cats and dogs only; ferrets will instinctively want to attack rabbits and small rodents that would be their natural prey in the wild).

Introductions between the ferret and other pets should be made carefully. The moment the ferret shows any sign of fear or aggression in the face of the family dog or cat, it should be removed from the situation and receive a raincheck for a later meeting. The ferret may come to enjoy these animals' company, or it may not. Respect the animal's wishes and those of the other animals as well.

Even when the ferret is fully acclimated to the house, the family and the other pets, this little animal must never be left unattended with children or other pets, or be left unsupervised outside of its cage. With a knack for making mischief and seeking out trouble, in the blink of an eye the ferret may escape or be injured, leaving its owner with feelings of regret over a sad situation that could have, and should have, been prevented.

A SNEAKY CRITTER

Never underestimate what this little creature might do. The possibilities are endless. That narrow space under the stove or refrigerator can sure look inviting to a ferret looking for new adventures. Some ferrets become adept at opening kitchen cupboards and even bedroom doors. Ferrets can squeeze through impossibly restrictive openings and master skills you would assume are possible only for humans. Curiosity, they say, killed the cat, and it certainly can do a job on the ferret, as well.

But of course there is much joy to be had from this creature's talents, too. Rarely will you find a pet that so passionately celebrates life.

Ferrets will tunnel into any rug or blanket they happen to see, or they may be content simply to remain underfoot. They will wiggle into furniture or hide under beds, where they will happily curl up for afternoon naps. They will hang on mini-blinds and attempt to climb up drapes and screen doors, which are activities that must be forbidden, for, despite their similarities to cats, ferrets can easily fall from these vertical surfaces and injure themselves.

Ferrets will hide food everywhere and anywhere, dig in plants and hide toys (which may be valuable items that belong to you) in nooks and crannies where they can never be found. They may even be inclined to burrow under the covers of their owner's bed and bite the toes they find there. For obvious reasons, many an owner has outfitted a gregarious pet ferret with a lightweight cat collar, complete with a bell to alert the family to the animal's whereabouts, and an identification tag, should the ferret escape out an open door or window.

In the midst of activity is where the ferret wants to be, whether that means jumping up to investigate the items in the purse sitting on a guest's lap, stealing pieces of a jigsaw puzzle the family is attempting to assemble or simply resting its head on its owner's foot as he attempts to cook dinner in the kitchen without disturbing his pet's rare moment of peace.

As far as the ferret is concerned, anything that belongs to its owner must surely hold great treasures: a suitcase full of clothes, a garbage can filled with crumpled papers and wonderfully enticing aromas, a closet full of boxes or a camera case filled with expensive equipment. All must be explored in great detail.

Needless to say, this type of activity requires some adjustment to the ferret owner's behavior. A ferret owner should adopt changes in habits and movements that, for the ferret's sake, become second nature.

While the ferret is out and about and having a great time, its owner should be blocking off the backs of large kitchen appliances, heating ducts and air conditioners, and checking the refrigerator, washing machine, dryer and dishwasher for a hiding ferret every time he uses them. Eventually, ferret owners will realize that almost subconsciously they have begun to walk with soft, careful steps through the house and to sit down gently on the couch. And that once-loved recliner that used to stand in the living room has been disposed of.

Of course the responsible ferret owner, now finding he is furnishing his home for his pet's welfare, embraces as gospel that when he is not at home, his ferret must be confined to its cage—securely confined. Given all that could happen to an unsupervised ferret loose in the house, that cage can save the animal's life.

FEEDING YOUR FERRET

Food is one of the ferret's favorite subjects. Active, energetic and playful, the ferret requires a great deal of energy to fuel its ambitions.

In terms of nutrition, the ferret's needs resemble those of a cat, as both require more animal protein than a dog. On the other hand, like a dog, the ferret enjoys vegetable material in its diet as well. In fact, it may enjoy just about anything it finds in its path. Because of the ferret's curiosity and appetite, a ferret owner must ensure his pet receives a balanced diet devoid of excessive treats.

Given its great protein needs, a ferret is best sustained throughout its life with a high-quality commercial dry cat food with protein derived primarily from animal rather than cereal sources. Although specially formulated ferret foods are now available, most owners still prefer those made for cats, especially those designed to facilitate urinary tract health.

Young ferrets, known as kits, experience most of their growth between six and fourteen weeks of age. They will thus eat like the proverbial horse during this time and require an abundant and accessible supply of food. Many owners feed young ferrets high-quality kitten food until the ferret reaches the age of three, after which they switch either to a regular maintenance adult feline diet or one designed for older cats which contains less protein, thus placing less strain on the ferret's kidneys.

Because a ferret may be inclined to eat many small meals a day to satisfy the callings of its speedy metabolism, the animal should have food available at all times. Consequently, it won't take long for the new ferret owner to understand the profound benefit of feeding this animal dry cat food rather than wet.

A pet ferret will usually get along with other family pets (except rabbits or small rodents, which it may consider prey), but be careful not to force the issue. *Michael A. Siino*

Dry food helps keep a ferret's teeth and gums healthy (as do periodic teeth cleanings by the veterinarian), and wet food can spoil or become unpalatable. But there's more. Given that instinctive ferret propensity to cache its food, the stench of wet cat food hidden around the house can grow to rival any odor the ferret's notorious scent glands could ever hope to emit.

Food, of course, must be offered in partnership with a constant supply of fresh, clean water. Food and water should be available to the ferret inside the cage and out. Heavy, solid food dishes will protect the food from spilling—and prevent the need for constant cleanups.

Ferret Food Favorites

Treats too, add to a ferret's fun, but while most ferrets are able to burn off excess calories through their daily activities, obesity is a danger. Treats must be offered sparingly—preferably as a training tool.

Cat treats, vegetable tidbits and yogurt treats made for small animals are special favorites of most ferrets, but guard diligently against anything sweet. Once introduced to the decadence of sugar, perhaps via a few shared licks of an unsuspecting owner's ice cream cone, and a monster is created. Ferrets can become raging sugar addicts with just a small taste, so prevent that initial introduction and save both yourself and your ferret much frustration in the future. Where any treat is concerned, practicing restraint from the beginning will help preserve the ferret's lean, lanky, sock-puppety figure.

Although a complete and balanced diet is critical throughout the ferret's life, as the animal ages, its protein needs will decrease somewhat. Still, the protein it receives must continue to be of high, easily digestible quality. The same is true of the ferret that is allowed to gain too much weight. While it may be switched to a light diet formulated to help over-weight cats lose some of the excess poundage, protein quality remains of paramount concern.

Obesity simply does not mesh with ferret character. Obesity can compromise a ferret's heart and lungs, thus hindering its ability to jump and leap and spin and wriggle its lithe body into the most unbelievably cramped spaces—activities that for the ferret, make life worth living.

GROOMING YOUR FERRET

What a dilemma it is that faces the ferret. It insists on being clean, yet curiosity often leads it into situations that leave it filthy, sticky and in need of a bath. The ferret is thus destined to spend a great deal of time cleaning itself just as a cat does. Owners may step in and offer some assistance in this endeavor, for even the most fastidious ferret could probably use some help to achieve that pinnacle of clean it seeks.

The ferret grooming kit should include a mild shampoo formulated for cats, ferrets or human babies; nail clippers designed for cats; a soft-bristle brush; a flea comb and flea-control products formulated for ferrets or cats (those for dogs may be too harsh for ferrets). Some owners also employ such ferret odor-control products as deodorizing sprays, believing that these, used in conjunction with descenting and frequent baths, can help keep the *eau de ferret* under control. With the increase in ferret popularity of late, owners can also take advantage of an increase in products designed specifically for ferrets.

The foundation of the grooming routine is daily brushing, which keeps the coat healthy, removes renegade loose hairs and helps keep shedding to a minimum during the annual transition when the heavy winter coat sheds to reveal a shorter, lighter summer coat.

Daily brushing sessions also offer the owner the opportunity to evaluate the ferret's all-around condition. Perhaps the nails are in need of a trim, perhaps the teeth or gums are in need of a veterinary cleaning or perhaps fleas have taken up residence on the ferret's belly. If the latter is true, the infiltrators should be combated just as they are when their host is a dog or a cat: Treat the animal as well as its environment (its cage and your house). Restraint is critical here. Use all flea and grooming products only as directed (or even less so), for ferrets, like any animal, can experience toxic reactions to such products.

If the nails could use a trim, which they probably will every few weeks, you are wise to recruit an assistant to help restrain the animal gently yet firmly during what can be many a ferret's least favorite activity. Assemble the clippers as well as a canister of blood-stopping powder—just in case. Trim only the tips of the nail and steer clear of the quick at the base, which, if cut, can bleed profusely and cause pain to the ferret, thus convincing the animal never to cooperate with this activity again.

A bathtime assistant can also be helpful, for not every ferret is a fan of water and shampoo. The sink makes an ideal and very accessible bathtub,

Ever eager and ready for play, the curious ferret will make virtually anything it discovers into a plaything. *Michael A. Siino*

enabling the bather(s) to wet the ferret's coat thoroughly with lukewarm water and lather it down to the skin. Make sure to rinse the ferret thoroughly, also down to the skin, to prevent the drying of skin and coat that residual shampoo can cause.

After the bath the ferret's coat must be dried completely, a process that is usually the animal's favorite part of the entire bathing procedure. Few ferrets can resist the grand game of rolling and frolicking in a fluffy, clean towel, a game that also happens to accelerate the coat-drying process and thus fend off the possible onset of a cold or other illness.

If introduced to bathing at a young age, the ferret should cooperate with the process fairly willingly. Make this a part of the weekly or biweekly routine, and you will soon discover that it can profoundly reduce any natural ferret odor.

FERRETS LOVE TO PLAY

If someone were to list what ferrets need most to survive, play would certainly appear prominently on the roster. The ferret is not a pet that can be locked away in a cage and ignored. Part of the responsibility of ferret-keeping is committing to daily sessions of fun. Ferrets are made to play, their physiques designed for movement, agility and action—often to their owner's amazement and sometimes dismay.

Ranking high on the list of favored ferret games is that of hide-and-seek. Innate mischief makers, ferrets cannot resist hiding items they find in the house and in their cage, or hiding themselves. The ferret with ample opportunity to do so is a happy ferret indeed, but the owner must be careful that it does not hide too well, especially in a spot that is potentially dangerous.

Ferrets are fascinated by the unexpected delights that they constantly discover within their environment. Everything is a potential toy, whether it be a traditional squeaky cat toy, a Ping Pong ball or anything that resembles a tunnel—including a bedspread, clothes in a laundry basket or a disheveled bathroom rug. Willing and able, they will try to worm and wriggle their way into any available nook and cranny, all in celebration of the joy of hiding.

Many ferrets also enjoy an occasional bout of mock combat with their caretakers, but owners beware. Ferrets tend to play rather roughly with one another. Caught up in the heat of exuberance, they may assume their human opponents are ferrets of a different form, and hence presume they may play as vigorously with them as they do with their own kind. A firm "no" and an end to your participation should break the spell and remind the ferret to practice gentler techniques.

To Burrow, To Chew

Ferrets are not rodents, and to label them so will elicit much anger from those who have allowed their lives to be dominated by these indomitable creatures. They do, however, like to chew at times, especially when they find a soft item in their path such as a squishy foam ball, a squeaky cat toy, or even lips, ear lobes or the septum of an owner's nose. You may thus be motivated to direct your pet's energies elsewhere, to more constructive toys that aren't quite so threatening to a ferret's intestines as soft rubber toys can be, or quite so personal and potentially painful to you. Use the ferret's endless curiosity to your advantage and provide it with a variety of playthings.

The ferret will joyfully tunnel into virtually anything, from the throw rug in the front hallway to the expensive quilt on your bed to the sleeves of your shirt. In the absence of anything else in which to burrow, it may spot its owner sitting cross-legged on the floor and run over to burrow into his or her lap or around those entwined legs.

PVC piping of three or four inches in width is another favored ferret toy, which may be set up both in the cage, where it serves as a burrowing tunnel and hiding place, or outside the cage as a fun exploration tube. In fact, some truly devoted ferret owners have grown so inspired by their pets' love of the stuff that they have arranged long lengths of it around the walls of their homes, creating winding, twisting, fascinating configurations that no self-respecting ferret can resist.

When Life Is a Game

Remember, all life and everything in it is a game to the ferret. There is nothing more wonderful than a perforated milk crate or laundry basket turned upside down with a hole cut into the side for easy access. Unless, of course, it's that expensive Persian rug in the living room, or your dog's favorite hard rubber chew toy, or those stacks of paper you thought were hidden under the bed, or that paper bag lying on the floor that not only makes beautiful crinkly noises but also provides a place into which the ferret can climb.

Some have likened the ferret to a kitten that never grows up. The ferret's natural play behavior opens the door to pleasant and effective training sessions.

If conducted in a tempting, patient and very positive mode, the ferret will view training as just another game in which it is required to participate in a specific role. Techniques that work with young puppies should reap success with ferrets, as well. Like a puppy, the ferret has relatively poor eyesight, for which strong senses of smell, touch and hearing compensate. It should therefore respond well to its handler's tone of voice, to consistency in commands and corrections and to treat rewards that will undoubtedly attract and retain the ferret's attention.

IN CONCLUSION . . .

The owner of a ferret must always remain at attention. One who does not have the time and patience to devote to so inquisitive, so agile, so incorrigible an animal, should consider another type of pet.

The ferret is a pet that must be watched constantly and demands a great deal of attention and interaction. A ferret can provide endless enjoyment and satisfaction to the right owner and endless frustration and regret to the wrong one. The true image of the ferret is not one of a temperamental, foul-smelling weasel-like creature, but of a very demanding sock puppet with an endless supply of energy. Those who do not care to meet those demands need not apply.

The strikingly beautiful red-eyed tree frog has evolved with toes engineered to grasp onto branches and other airborne surfaces with which it comes into contact. *David G. Barker*

CHAPTER 4

Princes of Pets: The Frog and Toad

Kiss a frog. You'll find a prince. No guarantees, of course, but it's worth a try.

As most of us well know, the fable of the frog prince has nothing to do with frogs, but it has withstood the centuries, immortalizing the frog, offering hope to single people everywhere and perhaps even leading a would-be princess or two to plant a peck secretly on the head of a nonthreatening amphibian just to make sure.

It is impossible to separate the frog and toad from the mountain of folklore that has followed them through the ages. Fascinating creatures with huge intelligent eyes, almost-human-like fingers and toes and a smile ever drawn across their faces, frogs and toads have long been featured players in fairy tales, folk tales, classic novels, film, television and cartoons, inevitably cast as crafty characters blessed with wit, humor and wisdom. We insult them by suggesting that to kiss them would be a most revolting act, yet we watch them, we read about them and we smile, barely acknowledging that by injecting them so prominently into our popular culture, we are announcing to the world how highly we hold them in our esteem.

We may not want to kiss a frog (the slime, you know), yet many among us are compelled to live with these lyrical creatures, to install them in our homes and in our hearts. That's not quite as simple as it seems, however.

As their more earthbound devotees understand, caring for frogs and toads in the style they deserve and to which are accustomed, is a grand mission. Make the effort and we mortals are ushered into a fascinating realm where the air is cool and damp, the sounds soothing and rhythmic, and the adaptations to nature are magical. And you don't even have to kiss one of them to gain entrance.

Frogs and Toads as Pets

	Light	1	2	3	4	5	Heavy
TIME COMMITMENT				🐸			
MAINTENANCE Grooming		🐸					
Feeding					🐸		
General Clean-Up				🐸			
SUITABILITY TO CHILDREN Ages Infant-5		🐸					
Ages 5-10			🐸				
Over 10					🐸		
SOCIABILITY			🐸				
EXPENSE OF KEEPING			🐸				

ABOUT AMPHIBIANS

Frogs and toads are amphibians, a unique group of animals that spend part of their lives underwater (usually for breeding and development) and part of their lives as land animals. Together frogs and toads comprise the largest group of the amphibian family. With members adapted to almost every kind of environment, their physical characteristics illustrate clearly just why this one lives in trees, why this one lives among rocks and why this one likes to burrow.

Most frogs and toads come into the world underwater, hatching as fish-like tadpoles that must then experience a metamorphosis. During this immaculate transformation they sprout what can truly be described as arms, legs, fingers and toes. Before our very eyes their heads thicken, their mouths widen, and their tails disappear. Meanwhile their lungs undergo a metamorphosis of their own as they prepare for eventual life on land. When the time comes, the newly morphed frogs emerge from the water, some destined to live in the trees, some on the ground, and some in both water and on land.

FROG OR TOAD?

From here, the lines blur. Determining what is a frog and what is a toad is not always black and white. Frogs typically differ from toads in that they tend to spend more of their time in the water than do toads—but there are exceptions. Toads tend to be land dwellers, well camouflaged to blend in with their surroundings, perhaps resembling a mushroom, a leaf or a stone—but there are exceptions. Bright colors are more likely to appear on frogs than on toads—but there are exceptions. Toads are typically more inclined to walk than hop, and their skin tends to be drier than that of frogs—but there are exceptions. You get the picture.

Once immersed in the world of frogs and toads, the importance of such delineations begins to fade. Each has a unique way of moving (some jump, some walk, some swim, some do any or all of the above), a unique way of hunting and a unique way of either blending in or contrasting with its environment, and each should be appreciated for its adaptations.

Toads tend to be land dwellers camouflaged to fit their surroundings, resembling a mushroom, leaf or stone. *David G. Barker*

We gasp at the agile dexterity and brilliant colors of tiny mantella frogs from South America (so colored to warn would-be predators that their skin carries toxins), and we stand in awe in the presence of the prehensile agility and expressive eyes of the White's and red-eyed tree frogs. But so must we appreciate the dignified demeanor of the bufo toad sitting statue-still, almost invisible among the rocks and vegetation that it has evolved to resemble.

There is some truth to the witty folkloric frogs and toads that must rely on their smarts to survive. The only defense these animals have against wild predators or sloppy human handlers is their natural camouflage, or, as is the case with some species, toxins in the skin that are effective only with direct contact. What all have at their disposal, however, is a repertoire of acute senses ever attuned to even minute changes in their environment, assisting them in both locating dinner and escaping impending danger.

SENSITIVE-SKINNED BEASTS

Yet another unique characteristic of amphibians is the fact that the animals breathe through their very sensitive, porous skin as well as through their lungs (although some amphibians do not have lungs). Critics who revile frogs and toads for being "slimy" just don't understand how critical that "slime" is to the animals' respiration, and hence to its survival.

The skin is a vital organ in any animal species, but in frogs and toads it not only acts as breathing apparatus and defense mechanism (assuming it is a so-called "poisonous" species with toxins in its skin), but also as a sponge to absorb moisture from the environment. At the same time, glands within the skin produce a mucousy substance—slime, if you will—that helps keep the skin moist and prevents moisture loss.

Losing that moisture, which will occur through the skin if the animal becomes dehydrated or is subjected to an environment that is too warm or dry, can be deadly. Knowing this instinctively, frogs and toads, and amphibians in general, spend a great deal of time under cover, seeking shelter either on the ground or, as the tree species can testify, among the leaves of trees. Most are then content to live by nocturnal rhythms, emerging in the evening to seek dinner in the cool night air. They know to protect their skin from long-term exposure to dry air and the bright and potentially drying rays of the sun. They know that to do otherwise is to die.

Handle with Care

The question is: Do these animals' owners know this? Some do. Those who don't must learn this lesson very quickly. They will then realize that these are not animals that thrive with frequent handling. Aside from the fact that

Although toads and frogs should only be handled on rare occasions, when it's necessary the hands that hold them should be moistened with water to protect the amphibian's delicate skin. *Michael A. Siino*

some, such as the poison dart frogs with their resident toxins, can irritate human skin, of more importance are the detrimental effects human skin can have on the frogs. Sensitive as the amphibian skin is, it cannot afford to be subjected to potential infections or chemical residues that may lurk invisibly on the human hand. Even human sweat can be an irritant.

While even in this so-called enlightened age, some among us persist in spreading the myth that you may contract warts from toads, the toad is far more likely to be harmed by a person than vice versa. Frogs and toads should actually be handled only as necessary. These are not cuddly pets who know and adore their handlers—handling is actually more of an annoyance to them than anything else—so respect their nature and respect their skin.

Precautions When Handling

When you must handle these animals, wash your hands thoroughly first. Rinse them well, then dry them well to remove soap residue, then wet them again in preparation for actual contact with the animal. A handler's moist hands will be more comfortable for the animal and for its skin. Carrying this a step further, some keepers wear water-moistened latex gloves for increased amphibian comfort and protection.

Go through this same cleansing routine between handling frogs and toads of different species and items from their habitats, as substances or toxins on one frog's skin may be irritating to another. You may also be wise to wear gloves when handling toxic amphibians, not because they pose any great threat to you, but because you don't want to feel the sting of irritation and unexpectedly drop or otherwise injure the frog. Wash your hands after handling them, as well, so you don't inadvertently transport a frog-borne toxin or irritant into your eyes or mouth.

In honor of the skin, the best way to interact with frogs and toads is to watch them. Set up a lovely enclosure, equipped with all the accoutrements appropriate for your particular species, just as you would do for fish in an aquarium, and enjoy. Your pets, if they could, would thank you.

SELECTING A ROYALLY ROBUST PET

Breeders. Pet stores. Your backyard. All of these are potential sources for finding pet frogs and toads. Where best to find them depends on what species you are seeking.

With so many pet frog species from which to choose, and so many of them being bred and thriving today in captivity, the choice can seem overwhelming. Just keep in mind that for many people, the first frog or toad is just that: the first of a long line of these animals that will share their homes in the years to come. Frogs and toads are quite addictive.

Some newcomers to the keeping of frogs and toads are most comfortable starting out with a species native to their home. This provides the prospective owner with the opportunity to study the animal's home turf ahead of time, thus allowing him or her to closely duplicate that environment in the home, and to provide the animal with vegetation and food items to which it is accustomed, as well.

A RETURN TO THE WILD?

Collecting a native species (there will be some that by law you cannot take out of the wild, so find out ahead of time) does raise one controversial issue that frequently circulates among amphibian keepers. What happens if you take a frog or toad out of a local woodland and something goes wrong (perhaps it won't eat, it seems unusually sluggish or you simply tire of it), and you no longer want to keep it? Do you release it back into its natural habitat?

It goes without saying that you must never release a non-native frog or toad into your local ecosystem. Such an act, while inherently cruel, will also disrupt the fine predator/prey balance that exists there, plus the newcomer

The bullfrog is a favorite to bring home from the local pond. Think carefully about keeping him, however, because he should not be returned to the wild once he's spent time with humans. *David G. Barker*

might contaminate the existing population of amphibians with an illness it picked up while living among humans.

YOUR AMPHIBIAN OF CHOICE

Whether you are considering a native North American toad or frog, or a more exotic specimen from the tropics, some preliminary education can help you with your decision and with preparing for the new arrival. Various species have different housing needs, and some even different dietary needs. It will be your responsibility to feed and house your green tree frog, your ground-dwelling toad or your passel of mantellas. The more you learn, the more you may want to change your mind about which species is for you.

Regardless of where you choose to purchase (or collect) your new pet, you should look for an animal that exudes all-around health, its eyes bright and clear; its skin clean and free of injuries, fuzzy patches, lesions or any suspicious growths; its movements fluid; and, if you have the opportunity to observe it, its appetite healthy. If you do happen to notice, say, a suspicious

Mantella frogs, such as this painted mantella, are becoming increasingly popular as pets. They are quite delicate. *David G. Barker*

patch of whitish fuzz on an animal you are inspecting, pass up that animal and any others from its tank, as well, as all might be infected with a contagious fungal infection.

YOUR FROG'S OR TOAD'S CASTLE

Obviously it would be impossible to present in limited space a treatise on the proper housing of all species of frogs and toads. Some require a woodland environment, some are most content living in the trees, some reside in the desert and some need water in which they can swim. The moral of the story, then, is that no one habitat design, no one castle, so to speak, will fit the princely needs of every pet frog or toad.

Again, research into your particular species of choice is critical. Only with such footwork can you learn where the frog or toad would reside in the wild (woodland? desert? rainforest?), so you might plan how to duplicate that in your home.

Some frogs and toads are aquatic, some are terrestrial and some split their time between the two. While the aquatic species usually require a setup very much like one set up for fish in an aquarium (filter system and all), most species will do well with just a shallow container of water in their habitat. A profoundly terrestrial animal may need only a small container, while a more water-loving species may be better off with its water in a larger receptacle, such as the bottom tray of a plastic flower pot.

While various frogs and toads require distinctive housing setups, some housing elements are standard for all. Security, for one. Aside from offering access to both land and water, the enclosures must be secure to keep these consummate escape artists inside. The top must fit tight, but so must it allow for proper ventilation, either through screening or a specially designed venting system.

The structure itself is usually some type of aquarium-style tank, often referred to as a vivarium or a terrarium. An aquarium-style structure of this type (with a well-ventilating top) effectively retains the humidity so critical to frog and toad health, and the tank can be easily cleaned. The tank may also be adapted to any species' particular housing needs, from those of a burrowing terrestrial species to one that lives in the trees to the aquatic frog that spends most of its time in the water.

How you outfit the vivarium, of course, depends on what the particular resident needs. All frogs, however, need a shelter, such as moist moss, a leaf pile, smooth driftwood and rock caves for hiding (a compulsion for amphibians protecting their skin's moisture), and any other naturalizing amenities you would like to add, such as plants for tree frogs. The closer these amenities come to simulating the natural environment, the more comfortable the frogs and toads will be—and the more content you will be when viewing what you have created.

As a variation on the aquarium theme, a tall vertical-style vivarium will accommodate the tree frogs' inclinations to climb. While they may enjoy climbing the glass walls of the tank, tree frogs will especially appreciate leafy plants for that purpose, especially live plants (with leaves that can so effectively be used for hiding). Plants should be rooted in separate pots which can then be buried into the flooring rather than planted directly in the vivarium substrate. This way you can easily remove them if necessary or exchange them periodically if you or your pets desire a change of scenery.

A simple, functional flooring material that is appropriate for most frog and toad species is sphagnum moss, which, while easy on the feet and a good medium for hiding and burrowing, also retains moisture to help maintain resident hydration and environmental humidity.

The benefits of a mossy floor should overshadow any thoughts of choosing an alternative that might be dangerous to frogs and toads. A frog, for instance, might ingest gravel on the floor of its enclosure—with dire results. As for the depth of the flooring, that depends on the animal. A large burrowing toad species, for example, will require a thicker layer of flooring than will a colony of tree frogs.

A more complicated flooring system that is gaining a great deal of attention these days is a layered design that fosters drainage and moisture control. This may be accomplished by first installing a grate on the bottom, followed by a layer of gravel, followed by a layer of clean potting soil or peat moss on top. If you can set this all up over a drain, that's better yet.

If this system sounds complicated, accept the fact that it's probably the direction you will be heading once bitten by the amphibian bug. The deeper people fall into this passion, the more obsessed they become with re-creating their pets' native environments. The results can be quite lovely: terrariums filled with plants and trees, all of which serve to showcase the frogs and toads which can be quite beautiful themselves.

Balancing Heat, Light and Moisture

Even the dark- and damp-loving amphibian needs light, and so will the plants in its terrarium. A fluorescent light installed above and outside of the enclosure (to protect the resident amphibian from coming into direct contact with it) will simulate natural full-spectrum light without emitting heat. Keep the light on half the day and off half the day to simulate day and night. Do not place the frog's terrarium in direct sunlight. That will lead to overheating and thus untimely death for the frogs and toads inside.

Frogs and toads are not at all tolerant of heat, as heat does, after all, draw moisture from skin. Even the tropical species will hide during the warm hours of the day and wait until evening to come out. Most amphibians should be kept in daytime temperatures at or around the mid-70s Fahrenheit (temperatures in the lower 70s are usually fine for most native North American species), so the room temperature of the typical household will usually sustain the appropriate temperatures within a frog or toad vivarium installed there. Supplemental heat sources are thus usually unnecessary.

Whether you choose a simple setup or one of the more elaborate designs, sustaining the correct moisture is a concern. Too dry and you risk dehydration; too wet, and you foster fungal infections and an all-around messy environment.

While moisture is important, at the same time, the enclosure requires adequate ventilation. For the most commonly kept species (not, for instance, the almost exclusively aquatic species), keep a clean water receptacle in the terrarium at all times (and change the water daily). Refrain from misting the entire enclosure with a spray bottle; instead, mist just a hill of moss in the enclosure every day or every other day to maintain adequate humidity levels in the atmosphere. This will also provide a damp medium in which the animal can burrow and hide if it feels so inclined.

As you learn more, become more skilled and, with luck, make more money to finance your grand schemes, you can set up increasingly elaborate setups. Designing the housing for your frogs and toads can become a hobby, and a passion, all its own.

A water source within a frog's or toad's terrarium will help keep the air, and thus the resident amphibian's skin, moist. *Michael A. Siino*

FEEDING YOUR FROG OR TOAD

Looks can be deceiving. Beneath that cherubic grin of the adorable White's tree frog perched on a branch, lives the heart and soul of a carnivore, a consummate hunter, an insatiable meat eater.

That large mouth wasn't bestowed upon the frog and the toad just for smirking, for smiling, for lending the animal well to cartoon caricature. Form follows function in nature, and nowhere is this more apparent than in the frog. The better to eat you with, my dear, the frog might say when confronted with a fly or a beetle it is soon to ingest. Only with a mouth that accommodating can these amphibians adequately capture and feast upon the prey that will keep them alive.

Within this particular realm of nature, the food chain is extremely violent. While frogs and toads seek their own live foods for sustenance, they must remain ever wary of those above them on the chain who would seek amphibians for their own menus.

No matter. The show must go on. And for frogs and toads, that means employing one of two typical hunting methods. Toads, for instance, especially those who are camouflaged to blend in with their surroundings, are likely to choose the "sit-and-wait" method, in which they sit and wait for the prey to meander by. A lithe, agile frog, on the other hand, is more likely to go after its prey, leaping forward and pulling it into that trap of a mouth with lightning speed.

And just what can these animals' keepers glean from this? Well, first, frogs and toads require live food. The movement of their prey stimulates the desire to eat and, consequently, the impulse to hunt with their amazing, quick-draw tongues. In caring for a captive specimen of frog or toad, then, you must supply the necessary food items to stimulate those responses.

The classic diet of frogs and toads can include a variety of items, and variety is what is usually best for amphibians. Ingesting the entire body of their prey as they do, they take in the appropriate balance of nutrients that their systems require.

While some species have very specific nutritional needs, most will fare well with commercially available crickets, mealworms, fruit flies, earthworms, beetles and any number of other insects that you can collect yourself with a fine-weave net you sweep over local vegetation. Larger toads have been known to eat pinky mice, and some keepers even collect termites from local wooded areas to feed their pets.

As a rule, frogs and toads can have rather voracious appetites, and most can therefore be fed small amounts every day, although the larger toads may be better off with meals offered every other day. Though not entirely necessary, you can serve the food items in a clean feeding dish, which may help you control the leftover mess in the enclosure. As another tip, once or twice a week dust some food items—namely crickets and worms—with a fine vitamin/mineral supplement powder formulated for reptiles and amphibians.

PREVENTIVE MEDICINE AND CLEANING THE CAGE

Within their moist environment, frogs and toads are prone to a number of conditions that, fortunately, can be prevented with diligent care.

First and foremost must be the maintenance of hygiene within the animals' enclosure. When that sensitive skin is exposed to unsanitary conditions, it can be extremely prone to fungal infections that will be exacerbated by the combination of a necessarily moist but unforgivably filthy environment.

Keep the terrarium squeaky clean. Disinfect the tank structure regularly, and remove any uneaten foodstuffs (i.e., uneaten insects drowned in the water) daily, which is also how frequently you should change the water. For aquatic species (which are more complicated to keep than terrestrial species), partial water changes should be conducted about every three weeks or so. As for wholesale disinfection, that depends on the animal, and the owner should be able to determine this simply by getting to know his or her pet and viewing the tank on a daily basis.

These animals' sensitive skin must also guide your cleaning techniques. They can be extremely sensitive to cleaning agents, so all resident frogs and toads must be removed from the premises and placed in a holding box or tank while you clean and disinfect their home. Once completed, rinse all tank surfaces and newly cleaned furnishings thoroughly of chemical residues, and dry the surfaces well before bringing the animals back in.

Although you can remove soiled sections of flooring daily, there is no set guideline on how frequently you should change the entire substrate of your pet's enclosure. This timeline will often be dictated by the number of animals you are housing together (the layered method with the drainage it provides will not have to be changed as frequently as traditional setups). Do remember, however, that the moss that is so ideal for so many species may not appear soiled even if it is.

Which brings us to the subject of handling. These are not pets you can remove from their home for a rousing game of fetch or a do-it-yourself tour of the homestead at large. As a rule, most frogs and toads, especially the tiny, delicate frog species, are safer and more secure in their enclosures. View them as consummate homebodies and allow them the luxury of remaining in their preferred digs.

The skin of the strawberry poison dart frog contains substances that can prove irritating to both would-be predators and unsuspecting owners. *David G. Barker*

Keeping your frog's environment clean, handling the frog properly and feeding it what it needs will all help prevent illness. *David G. Barker*

When you do handle these animals, as we have seen, your hands should be clean and moist, and perhaps even covered with moistened gloves. Most are safely picked up with a scooping motion either underneath their bodies or lifted gently with support behind their front legs. Support the body carefully to prevent injury and escape, the latter of which can be a challenge when you are handling a species known for its jumping ability.

A superior handling option might be a popular practice that protects the animal's skin and guards against injury. When you need to remove a frog or toad from its habitat, which you will for house cleaning or a trip to the veterinarian, try herding the frog or toad gently from behind into a holding box in which you have placed a clump of moistened moss.

Do the same thing if you will be traveling longer distances with your pet. Outfit a glass jar or a plastic box (with well-fitting top) with some moistened moss, perhaps even some leaves, for hiding places, and punch holes in the top for ventilation. There you have it: a safe and comfortable traveling container.

Keeping the environment clean and observing sound handling protocol can prevent illness, but even the well-cared-for amphibian can still sustain health problems.

Injury can result when two toads squabble over territory or a tree frog rubs up against a sharp object. Injury can lead to fungal infection, evident in a whitish, fuzzy growth on the skin. Fungal infections must be treated, preferably with assistance from a veterinarian skilled in the care of amphibians. The vet can prescribe a topical antibiotic, while you at home should thoroughly clean and disinfect the frog's environment (within an unsanitary environment, the condition will never be corrected), and ensure that the patient remains isolated from all other amphibians until it is cured.

Given the risks of secondary infection from injury, you are wise to evaluate cohabitation of frogs and toads carefully. While many species do well when housed solo, some enjoy group living and are devoutly social beings, evident in the obviously intricate communication systems they have developed. But others—say, two male bullfrogs in cramped quarters—may want nothing to do with each other, sentiments that could lead to cannibalism.

Even if you are keeping some of the more social frogs, make sure they are of like sizes and species so you won't wake up one morning to find that your larger pets have made an unplanned midnight snack of the smaller ones. A good rule of thumb with bullfrogs is to assume that they will eat just about anything, and must thus be housed alone.

Maintaining a clean amphibian environment, preventing situations that will lead to domestic violence, ensuring that habitat furnishings present no sharp edges to cut that delicate amphibian skin and isolating newcomers for several weeks to watch for potentially contagious illnesses that might affect an existing amphibian population, are easy steps one may take to protect frogs and toads from illness and injury. If the worst does occur, call the veterinarian.

Once upon a time many a veterinarian would have laughed at the client who brought a frog in for treatment, but not anymore. Today more veterinarians are specializing in the care of exotic pets, and even frogs and toads are benefiting from this development.

The spiny-backed, long-snouted hedgehog is a common sight in English gardens, and an animal immortalized in Lewis Carroll's classic, *Alice's Adventures in Wonderland.*
Michael A. Siino

CHAPTER 5

Fresh From the Garden: The Hedgehog

A love of gardens is a characteristic that is profoundly British, evident in the many fine examples of gardens we find in that country, and the devotion with which their keepers tend them. But just what is it that inspires those British gardeners so? Sure, the blossoms and the herbs are a draw. No doubt the serenity of the place is, as well, but there must be more.

There is.

Within these garden walls, snuffling through the hedges, investigating what hides behind the leaves, there waddles a wry, unique little creature covered with spines that itself elicits a great deal of attention and devotion from those British gardeners. That creature is the hedgehog.

A GARDENER'S BEST FRIEND

Spot a spiny-backed hedgehog trundling among the carefully cultivated vegetation in search of a dinner of insects, and you will be struck by its bright eyes, its tiny black nose and a delicate face that may be described only as precious. Is it any wonder that this animal has for centuries enjoyed such a devoted following of humans within the context of the British garden?

The story might be dif ferent if hedgehogs were vegetarians and competed with humans for ownership of the garden, munching on the plants and flowers rather than just moving among them. But as a very effective insectivore, this animal's presence enhances the health of the garden by keeping pests in

The Hedgehog as a Pet

	Light	1	2	3	4	5	Heavy
TIME COMMITMENT				🦔			
MAINTENANCE Grooming			🦔				
Feeding					🦔		
General Clean-Up					🦔		
SUITABILITY TO CHILDREN Ages Infant-5		🦔					
Ages 5-10			🦔				
Over 10					🦔		
SOCIABILITY					🦔		
EXPENSE OF KEEPING				🦔			

check. It's hardly surprising then that this charming little fellow we call the hedgehog meanders about taking for granted the warm welcome that originally brought it to this place that now claims it as its own.

AN ANCIENT PET

Like the presence of squirrels in the United States, hedgehogs are common sights in Britain, and have been for centuries. There they have remained fixtures since Roman times, charming generations of both the native people and those who navigated the channel from all corners of the European continent to cultivate and at times conquer the island nation. Legend has it that even America's own Groundhog Day actually had its start in Britain as Hedgehog Day. Nocturnal creatures by nature, hedgehogs were presumed, however dubiously, to possess the power to predict the weather by way of the moon.

Yet despite such an illustrious regional heritage, hedgehogs are in fact native not to the British Isles, but to warmer regions of Africa and Asia. Nevertheless, no matter what continent or nation seeks to claim them, hedgehogs attract a strong following wherever they travel. And now their travels have brought them to America, not to take up garden residence but, rather, to a new niche as housepets.

They were used as croquet balls in *Alice's Adventures in Wonderland*. One figured prominently in the tales of Beatrix Potter. Images of hedgehogs are enmeshed in human culture, the fond ruminations not only of British gardeners, but of artists and writers, as well.

No one, it seems, is immune from the charms of the hedgehog, yet while most people who reside beyond its English stomping ground have some idea of what a hedgehog looks like, few have seen one in person, or can even fathom the concept of keeping them as pets. One look, and you believe it must be some type of porcupine, certainly an inappropriate—not to mention dangerous—animal to keep as a pet. Right?

Well, no. But success in this field depends on the people looking to own them.

ABOUT THE AFRICAN PYGMY HEDGEHOG

Of the many hedgehog species now found in the warmer regions of the earth, the one commonly kept as a pet today is the African pygmy hedgehog, a somewhat top-heavy-looking animal that grows to about six to eight inches in length and weighs about one pound. These animals, which are native to the African savanna, are not considered the most intelligent creatures on earth, yet they are heralded as sweet, docile pets that should live as long as eight years (and perhaps longer) in captivity.

This unusual-looking animal that appears to move gracefully in its seemingly awkward, lumbering gait, may be found in a variety of colors, the names of which, though to date are not standardized, include white, black, cream and snowflake. Most hedgehogs, however, present a salt-and-pepper appearance—and a decidedly attractive appearance at that. So frequently do pet hedgehogs hear exclamations of delight over their appearance, most must surely believe their names to be "So cute" or "Adorable."

The epitome of cute, the hedgehog is known for bright eyes, rounded ears and a repertoire of sounds that can range from the purr of the contented hedgehog, to the chirp of the young, to the huff and chuff of the irritated or prematurely awakened, to the scream of the frightened or hurt. The hedgehog's signature pointed snout tipped by a small black nose are the manifestations of a keen sense of smell that assists the hedgehog, particularly the wild or garden-dwelling hedgehog, in its daily quest for sustenance or for new and exciting objects it hopes to find in its path during its nocturnal wanderings.

The salt-and-pepper colored hedgehog grows to about six inches in length, weighs about one pound and can live as long as eight years in captivity. *Michael A. Siino*

Not to be mistaken for any other type of animal, the hedgehog is distinct for the stiff, prickly spines that grow from its forehead, down its back and at each side. These are sharp, hair-like growths that first appear when the hedgehog is born as soft hair-like spines, ultimately making way for the sturdier adult models as the hedgehog matures.

Unlike a porcupine, the spines of the hedgehog will not come out in your hand when you touch them, but they do act as an effective defense mechanism. The moment the hedgehog feels frightened or threatened in any way, it can, thanks to a layer of specially engineered muscle beneath the spines, roll itself up in a ball. Now a dense, impenetrable fortress of spines, it is hardly an inviting subject for a biting predator. Its role as fictional croquet ball aside, if it is being cared for by people who respect its desire for quiet, kind handling, the captive hedgehog should not generally feel the need to protect itself in this way.

AN UNUSUAL HABIT

Another hedgehog practice of which the new hedgehog owner should be aware is the odd habit of self-anointing. The unprepared who have never even heard of self-anointing are sure to find it shocking the first time their pets partake of this interesting, and rather mysterious, ritual.

Little is known about the whys and wherefores of self-anointing, but it is generally believed that when a hedgehog ambles upon a strange or unusual smelling object in its path, it may become obsessively intrigued with the item. So inspired, it may begin to lick the object, chew it, taste it, and in doing so, begin to salivate profusely.

As the saliva—and the animal's excitement—build, the hedgehog swings its head from side to side and flings the now-frothy saliva onto the spines of its back. Why? No one is quite sure. It may be a supplementary protective measure against predators. It may be a mating ritual. All we know is that it is quite fascinating, not to mention unique, to the animal world.

LOW-MAINTENANCE PETS

Despite its rather exotic appearance, structure and behavior, the hedgehog is really a relatively low-maintenance pet in the grand scheme of pet care requirements. Proper care involves providing the hedgehog with a high-quality, animal-protein-based diet to satisfy that insectivorous palate; a large, warm enclosure with temperatures high enough to suggest those it would find in the wilds of Africa; a dark, warm, secluded place to sleep during the day; and consistently gentle handling.

Some insight into the hedgehog's world view can further help to ensure a more peaceful living situation. Loners at heart, most hedgehogs thrive best when afforded a solitary environment, safe from other pets and even other hedgehogs. While female/female or female/male pairs may get along together, cohabitating males can, on the other hand, get quite quarrelsome and injure each other severely.

HEDGEHOG HAZARDS

As we have seen, humans and hedgehogs have enjoyed a long and fruitful association. The hedgehog can successfully take that association one step further from the garden into the pet household, but only if it is bred and raised to trust and accept humans. A hedgehog of such a background can grow into a curious, inquisitive little animal that enjoys handling by its owner and, within limits, exploring the world around it.

On a larger scale, not all individuals may live with hedgehog pets in the United States, for hedgehogs, like ferrets, are illegal in some areas. Also like ferrets, the primary fears blocking their widespread acceptance into the pet world revolve around the belief that if hedgehogs are released into the wild (which, unfortunately, unwanted pets too often are) they will wreak havoc with native wildlife.

Another obstacle seems to revolve around the fear of rabies—perhaps a valid concern, but in this case, one that is possibly rooted in misunderstandings. Those who do not know and understand the hedgehog may witness the self-anointing behavior, see that foam at the mouth, those seemingly erratic motions of the head, and assume the worst: The animal is rabid. Of course, that is not the case, but those who want to believe the worst are difficult to convince otherwise.

On the more personal level, hedgehogs are docile, friendly, clean animals that can be ideal pets for apartment dwellers or those who live in similarly restrictive abodes that, because of space or policy, cannot keep larger animals. Despite their docility, however, being the meat eaters they are, hedgehogs do have functional teeth and jaws. If they are frightened and deem biting to be an appropriate response, they will follow through.

As nocturnal creatures who rely heavily on their noses for navigation and sustenance, hedgehogs tend to get to know the members of their families by smell. A hedgehog may thus come when called, not in answer to its name, but because it is responding to a familiar scent, with which it holds (hopefully) positive associations.

HANDLING YOUR HEDGEHOG

Assuming hedgehogs do associate those familiar scents with gentle handling, they should be amenable to being lifted and held. This is true even when they are awakened during their daytime slumbers. Interrupted so, the hedgehog may first curl into a ball, but if handled quietly and gently, perhaps held on an owner's lap while it wakes up fully, it should uncurl and begin to explore its immediate surroundings.

If, on the other hand, you treat the animal roughly, it may respond first by emitting a hedgehog scream, and then surely roll itself up into that pincushion-like ball, leaving you to feel ashamed of your misbehavior and committed to rehabilitation.

Preventing inadvertent roughness and the hedgehog trauma it can cause can be tough with kids in the household, especially in light of the natural fascination these animals hold for youngsters. For obvious reasons, kids are drawn to hedgehogs, but they must be trained and supervised to handle them correctly. Delicate, sensitive animals that could either be injured in clumsy, squeezing, unskilled hands, or sustain a serious fall after biting those hands, hedgehogs are best handled only by experienced adults or by properly trained children under careful supervision.

Hedgehogs aren't crazy about being handled, though they can become accustomed to it if done gently and correctly. Some owners wear gloves when handling their pets.
Michael A. Siino

CHOOSING A HEALTHY HEDGEHOG

It goes without saying that when seeking a hedgehog pet, what you want is a healthy animal with a pleasant temperament. In other words, a hedgehog bred in captivity by people for whom health and temperament are paramount. Recent improvements in breeding have produced generations of hedgehogs that are better suited to pet life than would be their English garden-dwelling cousins.

While the goal of what you are seeking in this animal may sound obvious, it still must be said. Hedgehogs today are perched on the threshold of a potential revolution. Labeled as a trendy, up-and-coming pet species, hedgehogs, as well as would-be owners, may fall victim to breeders whose primary concerns are profits, not hedgehogs.

Skyrocketing popularity is not particularly positive or productive for any pet species. It invites too many people into the fold who are enamored of the status of having the latest introduction on the market, and nothing more. Unfortunately, such individuals don't always take the time to do their research, to learn how they can best care for this new and rather exotic animal. Some pursue this knowledge after purchasing the animal; others never do, and the animal ends up the victim.

Are You Sure?

Consequently, evaluating your own motives for obtaining a hedgehog is just as critical as evaluating the breeders from whom you hope to buy this pet. Hedgehogs are relatively easy to maintain and undeniably cute, so you might be tempted to buy one on impulse. Resist that temptation. Hedgehogs, like any pet, deserve an owner who gives the decision forethought. They will not benefit from being seen as novelties.

Once you have invested this necessary forethought and come up with the honest conclusion that you must have a hedgehog, find out if you are allowed to have a hedgehog in your area. To obtain one in an area where hedgehogs are illegal is to invite trouble down the road should your secret be discovered.

A good breeder can be a valuable resource when you are gathering information and perhaps even when you are determining whether a hedgehog is right for you. Clues that a breeder is honest and is operating with ethical motivations are an emphasis on temperament, a desire to talk endlessly about the care requirements of hedgehogs and an obvious familiarity with each of the hedgehogs he or she has available (special likes and dislikes, unusual behaviors, etc.). Such breeders are typically members of the North American Hedgehog Association (listed in the Appendix), which runs a Registered Breeder Program among member breeders and can direct would-be owners to those member breeders for pets. You may also find good breeders at local fairs and pet shows.

Looking Closely and Honestly

When choosing a particular hedgehog, keep in mind that a young hedgehog will adapt best to its new home between six to ten weeks of age; any younger, and the combined experience of weaning and entering a new home can be too traumatic for the animal. Beyond age, look for the general signs of good hedgehog health: clear breathing; bright, clear eyes; a clean nose; and a body weight that is appropriate for the hedgehog's size. Don't worry if you notice minimal signs of a dandruff-like substance between the spines.

Hedgehogs raised in a clean environment should have no trouble meeting the criteria of a healthy specimen. On the other hand, within a cold

When stressed the hedgehog will roll itself into a spiny ball, a valuable protection reflex when encountering potential predators—or boisterous owners. *Michael A. Siino*

environment, or one in which cleanliness is not maintained, hedgehogs can develop such problems as respiratory illness or fungal infections of the feet. They may also attract parasites, both internal and external.

Of equal importance to health is the hedgehog's temperament. Look to the handler for some clues. Watch for the use of gloves. A breeder, familiar as he or she should be with the animals, should not feel the need to don gloves to handle the fruits of his or her breeding program. The need to do so may indicate a lack of socialization among the stock.

While most would-be owners would prefer purchasing their pets directly from a breeder, this is not always possible. Working with a still somewhat rare pet species, breeders are not widely dispersed throughout the nation. A pet shop may then be your only available source of a pet hedgehog.

Pet shops may have healthy, well-socialized hedgehogs available, but your evaluation process may be a bit trickier. In addition to feeling somewhat uncomfortable in handling the animals, the staff may not be much help in offering accurate advice on care or behavior. Take responsibility for this yourself. Educate yourself ahead of time, look for the same signs of health and hygiene within the shop that you would look for at a breeder's facility, and handle as many hedgehogs as you can. Insist this be done without a huge crowd looking on, and try to gauge the animal's reactions fairly.

Whether dealing with a pet store or directly with a breeder, observe the animal's individual responses to handling. Assuming of course that handling is done in a quiet, nonthreatening way that will showcase the animal's true nature rather than momentary stress reactions. Does it curl up the moment it is touched? If so, does it uncurl quickly or remain in a ball? The one that either doesn't curl or that does but comes out of it quickly is probably the better socialized hedgehog.

If the animal curls up in the gloved hands of an inexperienced pet shop employee, it is not necessarily a warning sign. Don't automatically assume in this case that the hedgehog is mean-spirited. The problem may be more with the temporary handler than with the animal.

Your Hedgehog May Choose You

Another important element in this evaluation process is observing the hedgehog's responses to you personally. Some hedgehogs actually choose their owners, exhibiting a profound dislike for some people, unmistakable love at first sight for others. Some prefer men, some prefer women, and some are content with everyone. Handle several and watch for the indicators. When you find one that you like, and it likes you back, you have a match.

FEEDING YOUR HEDGEHOG

Spiders. Earthworms. Snails. Slugs. Beetles. For the hedgehog meandering through a garden, these together comprise a veritable feast. The animal roots around through the vegetation, snooping under leaves and into thick hedges, relying on its sharp sense of smell to lead it to an unsuspecting insect, bird egg, perhaps even a baby mouse, ripe and ready for the taking.

Fortunately for many hedgehog owners, however, pet hedgehogs need not dine on such fare. They can, of course, and there are some keepers who insist that their pets stick to a traditional diet of live food, but for the more squeamish owners, or simply for those who prefer something a bit more convenient, there are alternatives.

In captivity, the hedgehog will thrive on a diet composed primarily of high-quality commercial cat food, dry and canned. Feed the hedgehog once a day, preferably in the late afternoon or evening when it awakens from a good day's sleep. Serve dinner in a clean, heavy food dish that cannot be easily tipped over or otherwise used as a toy.

A recommended menu consists of one tablespoon or a tablespoon-and-a-half of dry cat food (good for tooth maintenance) each day, supplemented by a teaspoon of canned cat or dog food (every few days), low fat cottage cheese, boiled or scrambled egg, chopped veggies and fruit (sweet potatoes, banana slices, halved grapes and apple pieces are usually appreciated), or perhaps a combination of these mixed together in a goulash from which you feed a small portion each day. The hedgehog may also appreciate a mealworm or two once or twice a week for a bit of traditional foraging fun. The animal's enthusiastic response to this may startle you.

Devoted Meat Eaters

It should be obvious that despite what an uninformed pet shop clerk may tell you when recommending a vegetarian diet for these animals, hedgehogs are devoted meat eaters. Though they are traditionally found in garden environments and will partake of vegetable matter, they will die on a strict vegetarian diet.

They also won't do well if offered too much to eat. Sure, they may comply and willingly clean their plates, so to speak, but the key to hedgehog health is moderation.

Because they don't spend their time and energies foraging for food, captive hedgehogs are quite prone to obesity—unless they decide to go on a hunger strike, which is not all that unusual, especially if you arbitrarily change their brand of cat food. If this happens, be careful not to entice the animal back to the feed dish with an overabundance of treats, or you'll end up with an overweight hedgehog.

If your hedgehog does put on more weight than it should, switch to a light cat food, which will be lower in fat and calories. Some owners, in fact, use this as a preventive measure, feeding their pets high-quality kitten food when they are young, then switching to a high-quality light cat food when the animals reach adulthood.

Of course the hedgehog must also have constant access to fresh, clean water, served in an equally clean water bottle. The water bottle is preferable to a water dish, which can lead to a mess when a gregarious hedgehog playfully empties the dish and saturates the floor of its enclosure, the bedding and everything else in the vicinity.

Which brings us to the topic of cleanliness, a subject near and dear to the hedgehog's heart. The type of foods this animal eats can, as we have seen, be rather messy, as can some of the animal's own eating and play habits. You then are charged with the duty of removing all uneaten food and soiled bedding from the animal's cage or enclosure every day. And while you're at it, watch for signs of diarrhea. A hedgehog with diarrhea is not unusual, the condition usually resulting from a diet that either is too rich or contains too much moisture. A switch to an exclusively dry diet for a few days should clear things up. If not, call the veterinarian.

SETTING UP YOUR HEDGEHOG'S HOME

The hedgehog is a homebody, pure and simple. As a nocturnal animal living among large, two-legged creatures who probably aren't, it must be provided with accommodations that allow it to pursue its nocturnal callings within a non-nocturnal world.

In a garden existence, the hedgehog is a home-loving creature that lives a relatively solitary life, making its home in thick, overgrown hedges; hollow tree trunks; vacated rabbit burrows; or crevices under outbuildings. Here it will build a soft nest and spend the daylight hours, safe from the glaring light of the sun, finally venturing out at dusk for its nightly forays.

Hedgehogs thrive best within an environment that offers them a sense of security. So ensconced, they are less likely to succumb to the detrimental effects of stress and, at the same time, will remain safe from potential house-hold dangers. As a hedgehog's owner, you are wise when designing your pet's habitat to heed this animal's love for a secure, well-protected home. It will be spending a great deal of time within this structure, and it should be made to feel comfortable.

Several options exist for the hedgehog home. Although they vary in style, standard to all is that they must not be placed in drafts or direct sunlight, they should foster ventilation as well as warmth, and bigger is always better. The larger its domain, the more content—and better exercised—the hedge-hog will be.

Aquariums, Cages or Kennels?

The first option is the regular glass aquarium. This should be at least a 20-gallon size, complete with a well-fitting screen or wire cover. While on the positive end the aquarium-style home prevents drafts, it may, on the other hand, fail to provide adequate ventilation and, if improperly placed, cause fatal overheating.

The opposite is true of our next style: the traditional wire cage designed for rabbits, guinea pigs and the like. This is a favored style among many owners who praise the ventilation it provides, but stress that it must be a cage with a deep, solid floor to hold the bedding in place, to accommodate burrowing activities and to protect the hedgehog's feet from the damage a wire bottom can cause. Some enthusiasts become so enamored of hedgehog keeping, they purchase custom cages in the quest to provide their pets with the largest, most well-ventilated domicile possible.

If this is the type of housing an owner chooses, the animal must be provided with hiding boxes for napping, and the cage must be situated in a part of the house that is quiet, warm and, if possible, somewhat dark. To

A well-ventilated dog kennel/crate provides the quiet, nocturnal hedgehog with ideal—and very secure—daytime sleeping quarters. *Michael A. Siino*

subject the animal to glaring lights, constant noise and commotion is to invite stress and the inevitable health and temperament problems to which that leads.

Another favored hedgehog home is an airline kennel or crate typically used for the transport of dogs and cats. Ventilation in this housing style is improved over that of the aquarium, because of the wire door in the front and the wire windows at the sides. Plus, its solid walls provide the hedgehog with that much-coveted quiet, security and privacy. Kennels are easily cleaned and easily moved, and they come fully equipped with a nice solid floor for bedding. They are also available in large sizes.

Accessories

Regardless of the style chosen, certain furnishings are required to truly make the resident hedgehog feel at home. First, the hedgehog needs a hiding box to which it can retreat and snooze during the day. This, of course, is especially critical for the hedgehog housed in an aquarium or wire cage where it would otherwise be exposed to irritating light and noise during the day.

The hiding box/bed can be made of either cardboard or wood, the only requirements being that it conceal the animal completely, be large enough for it to turn around in, and have a door cut in one side that offers the resident hedgehog easy access. A small segment of PVC pipe tucked into the bedding material is another nice amenity for a hedgehog, who can use this item as a supplemental hiding place or perhaps as an alternate napping location.

Cover the bottom of the cage with a three-inch layer of clean bedding material. Place some in the hiding box/bed, as well. The bedding makes the home cozier, and it also satisfies the hedgehog's natural desire to burrow.

The bedding should be pine or aspen shavings (don't use cedar, which can cause respiratory problems, as can overly aromatic pine), shredded or pelleted newsprint bedding (available commercially under several brand names) or hay. Remove soiled bedding as it becomes so, and change the bedding entirely about once a week or once every two weeks as needed.

Other Housing Considerations

In time, you will notice that the hedgehog has chosen one area of the habitat to use for a bathroom. This will probably be a spot on the end of the cage opposite its bed. Use this as an opportunity to toilet-train your pet, and place a small tray or pan filled with non-clumping cat litter in that spot.

Most hedgehogs readily learn to use the litter boxes within their cages, which will help make habitat maintenance quite a bit easier for you. A hedgehog is not likely to use a litter box as a cat would, gravitating to it when it is playing outside the cage, but the litter box, or, rather, litter pan, can make life within the cage a bit neater and cleaner. Keep in mind, however, that some hedgehogs might be inclined to use the litter box and its contents as playthings.

Most hedgehogs are very clean animals, content to groom themselves and enjoy a clean environment. If yours, however, happens to be of the school that takes great pleasure in tearing apart its home and rolling around in feces, you can assist in the grooming process by brushing the animal gently with a toothbrush.

Where you situate the hedgehog's habitat is just as critical as the nature of the structure and its contents. In homage to its nocturnal rhythms, the hedgehog's habitat should not be situated in the well-traveled parts of the house, those areas that experience the most traffic and noise. By the same token, this animal, which is most active at dawn and at dusk, can get rather noisy itself during its moments of high energy. Consequently, you probably don't want its cage situated right by the pillow of your bed, either.

When choosing the ideal location for your hedgehog's cage, remember that, for the animal's safety, direct sunlight and drafts must be avoided.

Similarly dangerous can be such locations as outdoors or in the garage, where you cannot control the temperatures. This can place the hedgehog at risk by subjecting it to excessive temperatures, both hot and cold.

Hedgehogs, hailing as they do from the warmer regions of the world, must be kept warm. They will usually do fine at regular room temperatures (70 to 80 degrees Fahrenheit) within their owners' homes, but in temperatures less than 65 degrees, they may feel the inclination to hibernate. If your pet must be in cooler temperatures, try installing a ceramic heating element like that used to keep reptiles warm. This will provide heat but no light, and it must, of course, be mounted where the hedgehog cannot come into direct contact with it. The best place for such a heater is outside the enclosure. Best of all, however, is to keep your hedgehog where the external temperature is constant, as it would be inside the house.

HEDGEHOG LEISURE TIME

Daily or near-daily handling is one way to keep the hedgehog friendly. Such sessions also have much in the way of satisfaction to offer the owner. These are not animals to be simply installed in an aquarium and ignored.

The physical benefits of play, exercise and social interactions to the obesity-prone hedgehog must not be underestimated, especially by the owner, who must accept the job of personal trainer.

The activity agenda designed to address both the mind and body of the hedgehog can involve activities as relaxing as just sitting together on the couch, or as rigorous as a quick spin on the exercise wheel, which some, though not all, hedgehogs enjoy using. Whenever the animal is out of its cage, make sure it is carefully supervised and remains within a safe, confined area.

Regardless of what particular activity you choose, always handle the hedgehog gently. This begins with the technique you employ to lift the hedgehog from its cage. The safest way to do this, explains hedgehog breeder Dawn Wrobel, is to scoop it up gently with two hands, one hand on each side of the hedgehog's body. Remain still, allow the animal to settle itself into a comfortable position, and carry on.

Choose carefully where you will put the hedgehog down. If you are going to, say, allow it to explore the dining room table or meander around your bed while you read, go ahead, but watch the animal carefully to make sure it doesn't fall off the edge.

While they do enjoy exploring, hedgehogs, for their own safety, should be allowed limited access to do so. Remember their own physical limitations, as well. Placing one up on your shoulder, for instance, can be dangerous for this dyed-in-the-wool ground dweller. The hedgehog is not a climber, it

You are your hedgehog's personal trainer, so to keep it from turning into a couch-hog, you can bring it out for some supervised exploring. *Michael A. Siino*

possesses limited agility and, on the shoulder of an absent-minded handler, it could fall and be injured. The bed, the table top or even your own lap are safer horizons for exploration.

Playpens

Another safe play area highly recommended by Wrobel is the bathtub. This can make the ideal hedgehog playpen. Plug the drain and cover the floor of the tub with layers of newspaper to protect both the finish on the tub and the stability of the hedgehog. Finish off the preparations with wads of crumpled paper, various and sundry PVC and cardboard tubes for hiding, and any other playthings your pet favors. Now just add the hedgehog to the mix, turn the lights down (a night light should light the room sufficiently to the hedge-hog's taste), and watch with delight as your pet rummages around safely and happily.

You can design a similar configuration outdoors as a temporary playpen. On a warm, balmy day, place a large bottomless cage out on the lawn in a shaded area (remember, no direct sunlight). Although you should provide the animal with a hiding box and some toys, it will probably spend most of its time snuffling through the grass, perhaps searching for worms or other surprises only a hedgehog would consider pleasant.

On such outdoor forays, make sure, of course, that the cage is properly anchored, that the animal cannot escape from it and that no other animals can get in. Even if its territory were so violated, it's likely the hedgehog would simply draw itself up into a ball, but it doesn't need the unnecessary stress of believing itself to be potential prey to a marauding predator.

The quintessential latch-key pet, all the quiet, undemanding hermit crab asks for is an interesting diet, a clean habitat and a selection of shells from which to choose when molting time comes around. *Michael A. Siino*

CHAPTER 6

Quintessential Homebody: The Hermit Crab

If there was an award in the pet world for the easiest keeper, the hermit crab, known more technically as the hermit treecrab, would be a powerful contender. Easy to house, easy to feed, this can be the ideal pet for people who have forsaken pet ownership because they don't have the time necessary to care for a pet properly, yet simply can't shake those internal pangs to share their homes with animals.

The answer to that longing just may be a fascinating little crab that moves from shell to shell in its lifelong quest for sanctuary.

Lest you believe the "easy" label slapped on the shell of the hermit crab means this animal has no personality, no flair, think again. The unexpected surprise hidden within that shell is the fact that the hermit crab is indeed a pet in every sense of the word. It lives by social instincts, it entertains both itself and its owners and it may even talk (in its own language, of course).

Welcome, then, to the world of the hermit crab. You may be surprised at what you find waiting here.

It's quite impossible for those of our species to ignore the trundling glide of the hermit crab as it meanders gracefully across the sand on spindly crustacean legs. Who would ever guess that this unusual creature, scavenging for food, grunting to its companions, would prove to be such a wonderful pet for people seeking a low-maintenance animal that is clean, odorless, undemanding and quite a kick to watch?

Few pet species are as adaptable as the hermit crab. Testament to this is the fact that no two are alike. Each is distinctive in appearance because they wriggle into any shell they find when the time comes to find a new one. The criteria for the new home are size and fit, not a standardized appearance that will mark all as members of the same species.

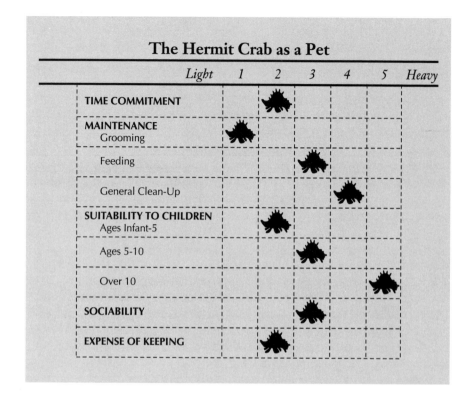

The Hermit Crab as a Pet

	Light	1	2	3	4	5	*Heavy*
TIME COMMITMENT		🦀					
MAINTENANCE Grooming	🦀						
Feeding				🦀			
General Clean-Up					🦀		
SUITABILITY TO CHILDREN Ages Infant-5		🦀					
Ages 5-10				🦀			
Over 10						🦀	
SOCIABILITY				🦀			
EXPENSE OF KEEPING		🦀					

Some owners of hermit crabs carry those differences even further with their pets, offering them shells that they decorate with jewels, paint, you name it. This doesn't hurt the crab, as long as nothing is applied to the shell that might be irritating or toxic to it. But if offered a choice, it's probably fair to say that the crabs would choose a more traditional, natural shell, one that didn't present quite so glaring a neon sign to would-be predators.

At first sight of the shelled crab, all you are likely to see is a shell just like any other shell you might see on a beach. Then the shell begins to move. It tilts backward and from underneath emerge spindly reddish-colored legs and an unexpectedly expressive, almost cartoon-like face, the sight of which makes you smile. Then you notice the large dark pincer claw in front. Rest assured that claw is fully operational, especially in times of stress.

THE WHYS AND HOWS OF HERMIT CRAB OWNERSHIP

No one knows for sure just how long hermit crabs live in the wild, but we do know they can live for a decade or more in captivity, the message here being that these can be long-term pets when cared for properly. The trouble is, too many land in homes where ignorance and/or apathy stand in the way of such longevity.

The purchase of a pet hermit crab is often done on impulse, especially in coastal vacation areas on the East Coast, where tourists flock for the summer. Collected from the beaches of the Caribbean, hermit crabs are brought to these coastal areas and offered to visitors at affordable prices or even free. Sellers make most of their profits on the equipment new hermit crab owners will need for the care of their pets. Unfortunately, though, the information these new owners receive regarding that care is often severely lacking.

Purchasing on impulse is not especially conducive to helping the hermit crab live a long and healthy life. Yet all is not automatically doom and gloom for these animals. Some of these new owners do provide their hermit crab pets with proper housing, food and atmosphere. These are very hardy creatures, after all, and they can thrive just about anywhere.

One "anywhere" that frequently plays host to hermit crabs is the school classroom. Installed as schoolroom pets, hermit crabs tend to fare better in this type of environment than do other species, particularly mammals and reptiles, that have a more complex set of care requirements. The classroom crabs not only fascinate the students, but also provide them with an opportunity for lessons on both responsible pet care and the wonder of nature.

So give some thought to the hermit crab before you leap. Once you give yourself the nod, find a reputable shop that carries them—which should not be too difficult as hermits are available in most regions of the country— and take a look. If the environment looks clean, the crabs lively and healthy, you may have found a pet that could be with you for the next decade or more.

HOME IS WHERE THE CRAB IS

If a hermit crab were asked what it wants most in the world, a home is probably what it would say if it could talk. For hermit crab owners wishing to fulfill their pets' every wish, a selection of shells of various sizes should fill the bill quite nicely.

Mother Nature did not provide the hermit crab with the ability to grow its own shell, so it must spend a good deal of its time in the wild searching for a larger shell, now a larger one, now a larger one still, as it grows through the years. In the wild it would find those left behind by other shelled creatures; in your home, you must supply the goods.

In a sense, the hermit crab is slave to a body that just won't stop growing. While for some life ends in the beaks of predatory birds or at the hands of ignorance, for others, the simple fact that they can't find a larger shell does the crabs in.

Rather social creatures, hermit crabs are happiest when housed in colonies with others of their own kind—except at molting time, when the molting crab should be temporarily separated from its roommates to prevent injury. *Michael A. Siino*

In the absence of a new and appropriate shell, a hermit crab will die. In the wild, desperate hermits have actually been observed squirming into bottles, chunks of coral, whatever they could find to protect their vulnerable forms. For the captive hermit crab, this need never be the case. When it's time to discard the old and embrace the new (about once a year or so), offer the crab a variety of shells from which to choose, preferably commercially available shells that are clean, sanitized and just roomy enough for the newly molted crab.

THE SHELL BEYOND THE SHELL: THE TERRARIUM

The shell is only half the story of the hermit's quest for home. The shell is actually the home within the home, for while the crab will be content within a properly fitted shell, it must be housed within a properly furnished, hygienically maintained habitat that will help it to live long and prosper.

This habitat can be a traditional glass aquarium or terrarium or a large plastic box. Regardless of the style you choose, the enclosure must have a vented top for security and ventilation, it must be escape-proof and the walls should be at least six inches higher than the largest crab housed within.

The ideal flooring material is sand, as that is what the crab would crawl upon in its native region. Two or three inches of commercially available sand free of microorganisms and parasites is a great substrate choice. You can also use clean aquarium gravel, but if the crabs feel inclined to burrow, as they often do, sand is preferable.

You may further decorate the habitat both for aesthetic purposes and for the crabs' enjoyment by anchoring such items as non-resinous driftwood or chunks of coral into the substrate. The terrarium will be easier on the eyes of observers this way, and the crabs may enjoy climbing on the furniture.

Providing an Island Atmosphere

Although hermit crabs are legendary for their hardy constitutions, the greatest threats to them usually revolve around issues of heat and humidity. It makes sense, doesn't it? Here we have a native of the Caribbean living on a continent where the climate and conditions, with the exception of a few areas, don't even begin to resemble those of those balmy native beaches.

Moisture. Hermit crabs must be properly hydrated internally as well as externally. They need water to drink and moisture in the air around them, the latter helping them to retain the moisture in their bodies where it belongs. If that precious moisture escapes from their bodies and the hermits become dehydrated, they will die.

While hermits need moisture to survive, they do not appreciate or thrive in a wet, sloppy environment. A system of several hydration techniques will protect the habitat and the crabs from losing that precious moisture without overdoing it.

First, the water dish. Install within the terrarium a clean, shallow-sided dish of water (change the water daily). This can be a jar lid, a saucer, a clam shell or a similar dish made of plastic or ceramic. Embed the dish into the flooring so it is easily accessible to the crab and safe from spills. While this may be used for drinking water, its presence will also help maintain a level of humidity within the enclosure's atmosphere. The same is true of our second method, a sponge saturated with water. While the crab will sip water from the sponge by actually squeezing it, the water within the sponge will also help moisturize the air.

You should pay attention to the hydration of the flooring, as well. Misting the sand or gravel two or three times a week should keep it nicely moistened and similar to what the crab would experience on a Caribbean beach.

Temperature. Temperature is another issue. A hermit crab should be housed in a terrarium that is maintained at temperatures ranging from 70 to 85 degrees Fahrenheit. Obviously this range just enhances these animals' reputation as easy-care pets, because these temperatures fall right in line with normal room temperatures of a typical household. Special lighting and heating elements are unnecessary.

An exception to this can be in the wintertime if you live in a house that is unusually chilly. But even this can be remedied easily with just a little sand.

Hermit crabs can actually tolerate temperatures as low as 50 degrees Fahrenheit as long as they have the opportunity to burrow into the sand. If, for some reason, your hermits are to be subjected to temperatures lower than 70 degrees, increase the depth of the sand flooring in their habitat to about six inches (gravel won't work). They may then dig in as necessary and keep themselves nice and warm.

Not too Hot. While maintenance naturally falls under the category of owner responsibility, owner negligence is often to blame for premature death in hermit crabs. Though they are tough little critters accustomed to a balmy environment, hermit crabs will succumb like any animal to overheating. Leave them in a hot car or exposed to direct sunlight (neither of which is unusual when someone purchases them on impulse while on vacation at the beach), or place their enclosure near a heater or radiator in the winter, and the immediate result will be dehydration and death.

Neat and Clean. Cleanliness is another responsibility. Keep the habitat clean. Given the crab's habit of burying food in the flooring of its terrarium, that flooring will demand the bulk of your cleaning efforts. Yet even this is easily accomplished. If you use gravel flooring, rinse the gravel out every week or two. If sand is your flooring of choice, replace it according to that same schedule. Remember, too, that the cleaning schedule will be dictated by the number of hermits you are keeping together and the eating habits of your particular pets.

LIFE WITHIN THE COLONY

If your ultimate goal in life is to breed hermit crabs, you are destined for disappointment. Unless you have an ocean and a beach in your living room, you cannot provide the components necessary to support the hermit crab's life cycle, in which the eggs hatch at sea and the hatchlings come to shore later in life.

While captive breeding is impossible, you can give hermit crabs a taste of the wild side by keeping several hermits together in a colony. These are very social animals that in nature often live in large groups. Take a hint from this.

As long as you're buying one hermit crab, why not purchase one or two more? With hermit crabs, the more the merrier. Housing several together fosters hermit contentment and increases your own enjoyment of these special pets, for watching their interactions can be fascinating and just as soothing as gazing at an aquarium.

THE MOLTING CRAB

Despite their communal natures, a hermit's molting time can place it at risk from its fellow crabs. Molting, which occurs about once a year, is a fascinating phenomenon in which the crab sheds the firm skin, known as the cuticle, that protects its body, revealing a new, larger skin that for the first few days will remain soft.

The crab is very vulnerable at this time. To protect itself until the new cuticle hardens, it will need to burrow into the moistened sand or into moistened moss you place in the terrarium for just this purpose. Keep the enclosure as a whole well-hydrated, too. Some keepers move the newly molted crab into a separate enclosure to protect it from other crabs that might try to attack it during this time. When it's less vulnerable, it may be safely returned to the colony.

When molting, a hermit crab may try on several shells until he finds one that fits just like Cinderella's glass slipper.
Michael A. Siino

When the hermit emerges, sporting a healthy new skin (and perhaps miraculously regenerated appendages that were previously missing), it will set forth in search of a new shell. Place several clean, sanitized shells in the terrarium, preferably shells that are about 25 percent larger than the crab's previous shell. Then sit back and watch. The hermit may actually try them all on for size until it finds the one that fits just like Cinderella's glass slipper.

In observing your fine shelled pets, consider yourself a part of the colony, too, and treat your fellow hermits with respect. You can take them out of their terrarium from time to time (lift them gently by the shell) and let them meander across a table, but keep them clear of dangerous situations and refrain from teasing them or allowing others (such as young children) to do so, as well.

FEEDING HERMIT CRABS

Hermit crabs are slow eaters. They don't eat much, but what they do eat should be of high quality and freshness.

Although they are scavengers that will eat virtually anything, this is not the guideline you should use in designing your hermit crabs' diet. Rather, look to our own species' nutritional guidelines for clues.

A basically vegetarian diet should both please and nourish a colony of hermit crabs. A smorgasbord mixture of corn meal, raw oats and perhaps some chopped fruit will do quite nicely, especially when held together with a bit of peanut butter (a hermit crab favorite). Hermit crabs will also take vegetables, but, given their tropical roots, they tend to prefer fruits, especially apples.

While hermits aren't picky and will eat what is offered, they don't know what isn't good for them. That is your job. Do not feed them bread, which when wet can clog their gills and suffocate them. The same is true of greasy foods. Grease isn't good for you, and it isn't good for your colony of hermits.

Hermit crabs have a habit of carrying uneaten food out into their enclosure and burying it in the substrate in a very dog-like manner. This habit will no doubt influence your decisions on what to feed your pets. Hermit crabs will, for instance, eat meat products, but this probably isn't an ideal snack. Do you really want a piece of rotten meat festering in the flooring of the terrarium? Probably not.

Another helpful hint for maintaining cleanliness and controlling odor is to feed your hermit crabs from a dish. This may be any shallow-sided receptacle embedded in the substrate of the terrarium: a jar lid or saucer works fine, but better yet are feeder shells. Available specifically for this purpose at pet supply and aquarium stores, feeder shells, usually small clam shells, are treated for sanitation, and when the crabs eat from them they will ingest calcium from the shells as an added nutritional bonus.

Don't be alarmed if the hermits seem to eat very little, or even if they take a vacation from feasting for several days. While they must continue to have access to fresh water at all times, fasting behavior is not unusual.

What can be a problem is if you fail to remove all uneaten food on a daily basis, thus inviting spoilage and parasites. Dry foods, being more resistant to spoilage, will of course cause fewer problems. Be vigilant in these duties, as well as your duty to clean and change the substrate regularly to remove any hidden surprises.

What would-be iguana owners must realize when choosing this unique animal for a pet is that those small, green lizards for sale at the pet or reptile store will someday grow to four, five or six feet in length. *Michael A. Siino*

CHAPTER 7

Dinosaurs Among Us: The Iguana

What is this fascination we humans have with the dinosaurs, the great reptiles that once roamed the earth? None of us has ever seen one face to face, and we know very little about their behavior, yet we stare at their bones for hours in our museums, we flock to movies that feature ferocious modern-day models of Tyrannosaurus Rex and our children have made dinosaur action figures a multimillion-dollar industry.

Perhaps the answers to these subconscious longings of ours lie in the fact that reptiles, both prehistoric and modern-day, are creatures that transport us back in time when the world existed without benefit of our human presence. It was an era that lives only within imaginations, when life was a daily struggle between predator and prey, our planet populated by creatures that were gone long before our own species was even a glint in Mother Nature's eye.

Our species may never have had the fortune of viewing in the flesh the giant reptiles that once ruled the earth (and we might not have advanced as we did had we been forced to compete for survival against such creatures), but we have been left some reminders of their reign—and more than just their well-preserved bones.

Today, in human households all across the country, there live populations of reptiles that serve to remind us of those giant creatures of so many millions of years past. Just visit your local reptile store and there, basking in the glow of a warm, well-lighted enclosure, you'll find the green iguana, America's most popular reptile pet—the dinosaur's most popular descendent.

The Iguana as a Pet

	Light	1	2	3	4	5	Heavy
TIME COMMITMENT						🦎	
MAINTENANCE Grooming			🦎				
Feeding					🦎		
General Clean-Up					🦎		
SUITABILITY TO CHILDREN Ages Infant-5	🦎						
Ages 5-10			🦎				
Over 10					🦎		
SOCIABILITY					🦎		
EXPENSE OF KEEPING					🦎		

THE IGUANA'S APPEAL AND POPULARITY

In the absence of dinosaurs that have for so long captured the imaginations of modern-day humans, pet owners are looking to the iguana to fill that void. Touching the collective subconscious of pet owners from coast to coast, iguanas offer their owners the opportunity to live each day with a creature of uncommon prehistoric beauty. Watch this animal sun itself on a large branch within its enclosure, and you can envision that same animal perched upon the mossy branches of some prehistoric tree, enjoying the sun and gazing out at a group of brontosauri frolicking in the swamp beneath it.

Every year thousands of green iguanas are imported to the United States from the species' home territory in Central America and South America, to answer the call for pet iguanas in American homes. Countless more are bred in captivity here in our own country, these lizards also destined for pet homes. The demand for these creatures is being abundantly met by the supply. But, at the same time, the public's understanding of how to care for them properly doesn't seem to be keeping up with the numbers of iguanas finding their way into American homes.

As more and more of the uninformed and unprepared become iguana owners, more and more of the unfortunate animals are suffering from malnutrition and improper housing, escaping into American neighborhoods, or ending up with rescue organizations and in animal shelters. This usually occurs when the iguana inevitably outgrows its owner's expectations and the novelty that brought it into the home in the first place.

Just as the dinosaurs met with some mysterious catastrophe that led to their sudden disappearance from the earth, in our own time, the dinosaur's smaller descendent is meeting its own catastrophic demise within American households. The cause? Unbridled popularity. Ignorance. Impulsive buying. The list goes on.

But despite the sad similarities, the iguana has life quite a bit easier than did its ancestors. The dinosaurs' fate was irreversible; the iguana's is not. We have the power to reverse the trend of ignorance and negligence that plague so many of these animals.

First, prospective owners inspired by the iguana's popularity can do iguanas everywhere a monumental favor by deciding to bring an iguana into the family based not on media portrayals or some misguided notion of how this pet might somehow enhance their own image, but on the facts of the iguana's care and character as a pet species. Only this way can we ensure that our nation's pet iguanas, the dinosaurs' legacies that live among us, withstand the pitfalls that inevitably lead to their premature demise.

OWNING AN IGUANA FOR THE RIGHT REASONS

Fact 1:   Iguanas must have heat and light to survive.

Fact 2:   Calcium and vitamin D3 are critical to the health and longevity of the iguana.

Fact 3:   Adult iguanas, especially male iguanas, can become aggressive, territorial and downright nasty when they reach sexual maturity.

Fact 4:   Not every iguana enjoys the role of family pet.

Fact 5:   Iguanas cannot live by lettuce alone.

Fact 6:   That adorable baby green iguana you see at the pet store that measures merely six inches from nose to tail can grow to be four, five or even six feet in length at adulthood.

Read and internalize these facts about the green iguana, and you will know more about the species than most people who take them in as pets today.

Indeed far too many would-be iguana owners spot the small, bright-green iguana youngsters, or hatchlings as they are called, frolicking among the branches in the pet store display, the lizards' eyes bright, their mouths almost

The iguana possesses a prehistoric beauty that carries its owners back to the age of the dinosaurs. *Michael A. Siino*

seeming to smile, and they just can't resist. They know nothing about the care of these creatures, which can be quite difficult.

The six facts listed above might have been all the deterrent a great many former iguana owners would have needed to dissuade them from choosing a pet iguana over, say, a pet kitten or a rabbit. A great many people these days are having to learn the hard way that despite its typically quiet nature and regal demeanor, this is a pet that requires a great deal of care—and specialized care, at that.

In the face of its immense popularity, the iguana is being marketed by people who either don't know how the lizards should be cared for, or by those who simply hunger to turn a profit. Either way, the results are not good for the iguana.

At the same time there are people who are deeply enamored of these fascinating lizards and are ever anxious to welcome similar souls into the fold of long-term iguana ownership. These are the same people who only half-heartedly joke in speculation about all the iguanas that are now either abandoned or lost by negligent owners into the great outdoors in regions with temperatures mild enough to sustain them, say Florida or Southern

California. Will these iguanas form feral packs and roam the countryside in search of revenge? Picture that image for a moment. Considering the great number that might be out there, it may not be far off base.

GETTING THE RIGHT IGUANA

Needless to say, it is the individuals from the genuinely dedicated camp from whom you should purchase an iguana pet. They know from experience that iguanas can make fine, often very tame pets for those prepared to care for them, and they will do their best to ensure their animals land in deserving homes. Whether they operate out of a pet store or their own breeding facility, they not only will be able to provide you with a healthy, well-socialized pet, but they can also be a valuable source of information as you work to provide the animal with the best care possible.

Your odds of success are greatest if you choose an iguana with clear, bright eyes; a plump physique, which suggests the animal is well-nourished and properly hydrated; skin that is a vivid shade of green and is free of lumps, bumps, lesions or discolorations; and an alert, lively outlook on life. Purchase this animal from a clean facility staffed by individuals who are confident in giving advice about their care and are comfortable handling the critters. The animal should breathe clearly and have no evidence of diarrhea within its enclosure.

As is often the case with reptiles, captive-bred iguanas will generally be superior as pets in both health and temperament to those taken from the wild. While there are no guarantees with any iguana, an iguana bred and raised among knowledgeable humans is more likely to be personable and interactive toward our species. And that is, after all, the reason most prospective owners look at iguanas when considering taking a reptile for a pet. An iguana that appears calm, docile and interested in its surroundings and in human activity is probably a good prospect. On the other hand, uncontrolled activity can be a sign of stress and a related predisposition to illness.

About Gender

Unfortunately, it is usually impossible to tell a male from a female iguana until the animal reaches about eighteen months of age. Even then, gender determination usually requires the eye of an experienced reptile veterinarian or herpetologist. This, of course, can prove a challenge considering that most iguanas are purchased as young hatchlings. Even as the animal matures, certain behaviors presumed to be male, such as head bobbing, can also be exhibited by females. One can only hope that, regardless of gender, with proper care the animal grows into an adult with a liking for humans,

Iguanas born and raised among humans are more likely to be personable than one that is taken from its native land. *Michael A. Siino*

and even if it doesn't, the owner will commit to respecting the iguana for its particular personality.

Iguana Individuality

This is not to say that all iguanas that appear calm and docile will walk on a leash or sit peacefully on your shoulder whenever you ask them to do so. Each iguana is an individual. Some will consider a romp on the iguana harness to be a special treat, while others consider this to be the ultimate indignity.

Misconceptions about iguanas are common, because most of the iguanas the general public meets are those that like people and enjoy attention. These are the iguanas who accompany their owners out into the limelight to serve as likable ambassadors of their species. Our species then makes broad generalizations about theirs, and assumes that all iguanas enjoy human contact. While early socialization and gentle, consistent handling throughout its life can foster people-loving attitudes in an iguana, experienced keepers know that there are just as many iguanas who would prefer humans to remain at a distance as those who crave human attention and interaction.

It may take a while to figure out which philosophy your pet iguana holds. Remember, too, that even the docile, friendly iguana, particularly a male iguana, can change dramatically when it reaches sexual maturity. Its hormones can cause aggressive reactions and territorial behavior toward other iguanas—and even toward its owner.

As an individual, each iguana will express its own unique personality, a fact that becomes abundantly clear to those who keep two or more of these lizards. Some iguanas like handling and family interactions; others don't. Some enjoy riding on their owner's shoulder around the house and relish a good scratch under the chin; others don't. Some enjoy sharing their habitats with other iguanas; others don't (which is fine because most fare quite well when housed solo). The lesson to be learned here? Get to know your iguana and respect it for what and who it is.

THE HEALTHY IGUANA

One fact is clear: Caring for an iguana properly and watching it thrive at its optimum health in a properly appointed habitat is one of the most rewarding experiences a pet owner can ask for.

One important step toward attaining this goal is to find a veterinarian who is trained and experienced in the care of reptiles, an expertise that will undoubtedly encompass the care of the very popular iguana. While locating such a practitioner may have been nearly impossible in many areas 20 years ago, that is not the case today.

In answer to the call for such specialization, and to the burgeoning popularity of reptile pets, the number of reptile veterinarians is growing, as is the quality of care and long-term good health these pets are enjoying. Your best bet, of course, is to find this veterinarian long before you are ever in need of his or her services. Making contact ahead of time will be a blessing in an emergency, or even when you just need a little help trimming those dagger-like claws that were engineered so ideally for climbing.

In addition to veterinary care, it can be rather expensive to keep a reptile in the style in which it best thrives. You will be required to create a distinct environment for this animal, an environment that is quite different from that of your home at large. While many owners allow their iguana pets free rein to roam their homes, these lizards do require homes of their own, as well. This domicile must include several important amenities, and the temperature must be maintained at a level quite a bit warmer than that of the typical human household.

Iguanas hail from tropical climates; you probably do not. You must therefore adjust a portion of your environment to meet its needs rather than forcing it to adjust to yours. While iguanas enjoy desertlike heat and sun, they must also have access to moisture, and they must be able to move out of the sun when their bodies tell them they have had enough light. Chalk the cost, time and maintenance of such an environment up to the accepted, normal cost and effort of keeping an iguana healthy. Ignore the need for specialized light sources, humidity and temperature gradients within the iguana's enclosure and you invite a dangerous downturn in the iguana's immune system and overall health.

As with any pet, monitor the iguana carefully and regularly, remaining ever vigilant for signs of any differences in appearance, behavior or appetite. Get well-acquainted with the animal and you will notice immediately a sudden unhealthy sound to its breathing; a dullness to its eyes; a dramatic lack of activity; the appearance of unusual lumps, bumps or abnormalities on the skin that could indicate a fungal infection, a parasite infestation or some other disorder; or the appearance of a misshapen, swollen-looking jaw that could indicate a calcium deficiency.

Exposure to natural sunlight is essential for a healthy iguana.
Michael A. Siino

Get acquainted with the iguana's normal skin color and variations so you'll know if odd changes occur. (Though usually bright green when young, an iguana's scaly skin can turn to more muted shades of greens, golds and even oranges as the animal matures.) Anything unusual is worthy of attention, for a budding health problem is better addressed at its onset rather than later when it might be too late or extremely difficult to treat.

Check the iguana's stools regularly, too. They should be smooth and uniform in shape. It's not pleasant to think about getting acquainted with normal droppings, but it is necessary if you are to recognize changes that may signal problems. Any changes that indicate a digestive problem require veterinary attention. You must never wait and simply assume that a suspicious lump or breathing problem will go away.

Most health problems in iguanas may be traced back to owners who are either negligent or just ignorant about proper care of this species. A related culprit is stress, enemy to all reptiles, especially to reptiles that have been taken from the wild.

Do what you can to keep stress to a minimum because a stressed iguana is more susceptible to illness. Keep the environment clean and properly maintained; avoid overhandling, especially of an iguana who doesn't particularly enjoy being held; and respect and accommodate the lizard's desire for privacy. Simply put, take active measures to reduce an iguana's stress, protect the immune system and prevent disease.

LIVING WITH AN IGUANA

When you first bring a new pet iguana home, give it some space and give it some time. Regardless of where it has come from, this is a new environment for the lizard, filled with new sights and smells. Give it time to get acquainted with its new digs free from unnecessary intrusions from the new strange humans in its midst. Don't overhandle the animal—or, better yet, don't handle it at all—for the first few days or even weeks. When it begins to feel secure, evident in a healthy appetite and basking behavior, it will acclimate more comfortably to new situations, surroundings and people.

Of course allowing your new pet time on its own requires that you establish its home before it joins the family. This involves simulating its native habitat in Central and South America, where a wild iguana may be seen perched on a branch basking in the sun above a pristine body of water, just as we envisioned it might do were it a fixture back in the dinosaur days.

While a glass aquarium-style tank of twenty gallons or so may suffice as home for a young iguana newly arrived in the household, what many a first-time owner either doesn't know or conveniently forgets is that these lizards can grow to be as long as five or six feet in length (males being the lizards more likely to claim the upper reaches of this range). Remember this when oohing and ahhing over that cute little six-inch youngster at the pet store. It won't remain that convenient size for long.

Of course the first home for that diminutive youngster will probably not be its permanent habitat given the change of size that will occur over the next few years. While you can move the lizard gradually into enclosures of increasing size as it grows, it is more economical to provide it with the largest enclosure possible from the beginning, preferably one of about forty gallons or so. This will provide the iguana with ample room in which to breathe and vertical climbing space in which to pursue its natural inclination to sit among the branches.

SETTING UP THE IGUANA'S ENCLOSURE

The larger the better: Remember this when choosing and designing your iguana's home. Most aquarium-style tanks are too small to accommodate a full-grown iguana; a large, domed, bird-cage-type cage with bars or wire properly spaced to prevent escape might provide a better choice. Better yet, and the option most dedicated iguana owners eventually turn to, are large custom-made enclosures with glass doors and a combination of screen and wood or fiberglass walls to help balance heat, light and ventilation. These are designed specifically for iguana care, with substantial height to accommodate climbing branches and built-in fixtures for safe and effective lighting. Such custom-made enclosures are usually available by mail order or at specialty shops, but their effects on their inhabitants are worth the effort and the cost.

Regardless of the enclosure style you choose for an iguana, you must be able to close and lock the door securely, preferably with a "pick-proof" latch to prevent escape. If the door or opening is on the top of the enclosure, as it will be in a traditional fish-tank-style enclosure, it must be sturdy enough to support the all-important light fixtures. Those fixtures are best positioned on top of the enclosure rather than within, where the lizard might come into contact with the hot bulbs or live sockets. A screen-lined wood frame provides ample ventilation and is an excellent top material. This is superior to glass, which will filter the light from the overhead fixtures and minimize the effects of their waves (see "Light and Longevity," below).

As important as the door design is the material you choose for the habitat's flooring. Several good choices exist, some of the best being newspaper, unprinted newspaper stock, butcher paper or paper towels; layers that can be removed every day when they become soiled by feces, urine and uneaten food. Some keepers use indoor/outdoor carpet (cleaned regularly and thoroughly, of course), while others recommend alfalfa pellets. All in all, flooring choice is a matter of taste, dictated by what is easiest for the owner to maintain. Whatever the owner chooses for his or her pet's habitat must be kept clean and be changed regularly to prevent bacterial infection.

Just as there are several flooring materials from which to choose, so are there others to avoid. Do *not* use sand, dirt, soil, gravel, walnut shells, crushed corncobs or cat litter as a substrate. Because these are rather messy and unwieldy, they are too hard to clean and keep disinfected. They can also be drying to the environment; plus a curious iguana can ingest these materials and suffer severe intestinal problems.

Accessories for the Tank

Of course there is more to an iguana's abode than merely walls, a top and a bottom. The ideal iguana habitat should be furnished with some staple accessories. All enclosure surfaces and furnishings should be smooth and free of sharp edges that could cut the iguana's delicate skin.

Hailing from tropical environments as they do, iguanas also rely on sufficient levels of humidity within their enclosures. This may be supplied simply by placing a small shallow dish of fresh water in the enclosure, which the lizard may also use for drinking. If the animal is receiving a diet rich in moisture, as it should from the ideal iguana diet of fresh, raw fruits and vegetables, you may never see it drink because it is receiving sufficient moisture from its dinner. Even so, place the dish in the enclosure one or two days a week, just in case.

Another method for providing moisture to and around the iguana—and one preferred by many experienced keepers—is to mist the iguana lightly with a spray bottle once or twice a week. The iguana may actually enjoy this in that it reminds it of life in the rainforest, plus it may subsequently be inclined to lick the water droplets off the walls of its enclosure. Everybody wins.

Like many an exotic pet, from time to time iguanas feel inclined to hide from the outside world. They cherish their privacy. Provide the animal with a small box in which it may hide its entire body. Cut a hole in one side for easy access by the iguana. This box will provide sanctuary for a stressed iguana, fostering a sense of security in the animal and enabling it to retreat when it no longer wants the eyes of the world upon it. Silk or live plants and branches may also supply partial hiding areas; the branches will also provide the perfect perch when the iguana decides to partake of another favored activity: basking.

No healthy, self-respecting iguana can ignore that urge to bask in the sunlight or beneath the basking light set up above its habitat. Offer the animal a choice with a variety of branches arranged at various levels. These branches must of course be free of pesticides, parasites or fungal growths, and they must be anchored securely to the floor and the sides of the enclosure to prevent slippage and possible subsequent injury to the lizard.

Your iguana's habitat should be set up to provide sufficient light, heat and places to perch—with no sharp edges. *Michael A. Siino*

Depending on the size of the enclosure—and remember, bigger is better—you can accentuate your iguana's miniature rainforest, and make it feel more and more at home, with large rocks, hollow logs and chunks of driftwood, the latter of which is marketed in a sanitized, climbable, perchable form for climbing lizards.

What many keepers refer to as a sun cage—a temporary outdoor enclosure for an iguana—may also be considered a necessary accessory for this animal. While the purpose of this cage is to offer the animal an opportunity to bask a while in the sunlight, you must not use a glass aquarium, which will overexpose the lizard to heat and sunshine.

The sun cage must be just that: a cage with plenty of ventilation. In addition to access to sunshine, the sun cage must also provide the animal with access to shade; be constructed of a webbed wire or other secure, ventilating material; and it must be just as escape-proof as the main enclosure with all the furnishings the iguana would have there, as well.

The iguana should spend time in the sun cage or outdoor enclosure only when the weather is ideal for that—not too warm, not too cool. Keep in mind when placing your iguana in the sun cage that the position of the sun will change and alter the shade as the day progresses. Plan accordingly.

LIGHT AND LONGEVITY

Most of us have at one time or another seen a lizard, any lizard, large or small, basking in the sun on a rock. But what many of us may not realize when witnessing this sight is the fact that there is a method to this animal's madness. It basks not just because the heat feels warm and comforting on its skin, but because it must do so to survive.

Without an appropriate light source, meaning one that mimics the natural sunlight to which the iguana would be exposed in the wild, the animal's body will not be able to assimilate nutrients, especially vitamin D3 and calcium, from its diet properly. Heat is equally critical, its job being to stimulate the iguana's appetite and digestion.

How we provide that light and heat is a subject of great debate and discussion among those passionate about iguanas. This is one of the most critical elements involved in the long-term health and well-being of these lizards, and one of the subjects about which neophyte owners are often most ignorant. In other words, many an iguana has perished in the hands of owners who did not, for whatever reason, provide their pets with appropriate light and heat.

But you need not fall into that trap. In most cases a simple combination lighting system should provide an iguana with all the heat and light it needs. Because iguanas are diurnal creatures that prefer lighting that comes from above just as it would from the sun, the lights of its enclosure should be positioned on top and outside of its enclosure.

Most experienced iguana keepers agree that despite some claims to the contrary, adequate heat and light cannot be provided with a single light source. The best combination is a fluorescent light tube for the ultraviolet rays so critical to reptile metabolism, coupled with a heat-giving incandescent light positioned at one side of the enclosure for heat and basking. Some commercially available enclosures are designed specifically for this lighting partnership; others require the owner to use a little design ingenuity.

Although the florescent light does not emit heat, it quietly performs miracles within the iguana's system. Without those ultraviolet (UVA and UVB) rays available either from fluorescent lighting or the sun, the animal's system cannot synthesize vitamin D3, which is directly related to its storage and use of calcium and phosphorus. If the iguana goes too long with inadequate lighting, and/or insufficient calcium in its diet, the owner will soon notice the telltale swollen jaw that indicates the onset of metabolic bone disease. In this disease the iguana's body, in the absence of sufficient calcium, uses its own bones for its calcium source.

While iguanas should receive a vitamin D3 supplement as part of their diets, this alone will not suffice. Lighting is all-important, as is its management. Do not position a fixture so that the light must pass through glass or plastic. This will diffuse the light and weaken its effects, as will excess use of a single bulb. Change the bulb once or twice a year before it burns out, as it will lose its punch long before it fades away.

Through the years herpetologists have become quite skilled in cracking the code of the ideal synthetic sunlight system for the iguana, yet we must not underestimate the power of the real thing. Artificial light does the job, but every iguana needs to bask in real sunlight from time to time.

TAKING YOUR IGUANA WITH YOU

The well-built portable sun cage, positioned for sun as well as shade, offers an ideal vehicle for basking in the sun. Another option, but one that depends solely on the iguana's amenability to it, is an outing on a leash. If your pet is willing to be harnessed in one of the leashes designed especially for iguanas, great. It can ride upon your shoulder as you take a walk or visit with friends, or sit with you in the grass as you read beneath a tree, safely restrained as it soaks up the sun's healthy rays. Do not force the issue. Some iguanas want no part of the leash and should be respected for those sentiments.

ADVICE ABOUT TEMPERATURES

As for heat, this too can be tricky. Your goal is not only to maintain appropriate temperatures, but also to provide the animal with a temperature gradient that will allow it to warm and cool itself according to its own wishes.

Iguanas, like all reptiles, are ectothermic. Their body temperatures, which cannot be generated internally, are completely at the mercy of the temperatures within their environment. With bodies designed to absorb heat from their surroundings, iguanas in the wild remain sheltered at night to guard against the cool night air, then emerge in the daytime to warm their bodies with the sun and the warm air. They migrate between warmth and shade all day, so you must provide them with the opportunity to do the same in captivity.

Temperature requirements for iguanas are quite specific. During the daytime, one end of the enclosure should be warmed to about 80 to 83 degrees Fahrenheit, which rises gradually to a maximum of about 95 to 100 degrees

Some iguanas will ride along on their owner's shoulder, but others prefer to be left alone. Respect your pet for the particular personality it was born with.
Michael A. Siino

on the opposite end directly under the heat lamp, the latter temperature offering the perfect spot for basking.

At night, when the lights are turned off, for this animal prefers its nights dark just as they would be in the wild, the temperature may dip down to about 75 degrees. As a basic guideline, leave the lights on for twelve to fourteen hours a day; to leave them on full-time in an effort to maintain heat is to confuse the iguana both psychologically and physically.

That incandescent light positioned at the top of the basking end of the enclosure should help facilitate the heat gradient (with basking surfaces positioned conveniently beneath it, of course), yet some keepers prefer to add some additional heat sources as well, especially during the night when the heat-producing light source is turned off.

One heating option that is frequently recommended to fledgling iguana owners (usually by equally fledgling iguana sellers) is the hot rock, a flat rock formation that houses an electrical heating element. While it sounds well and good, a great many experienced reptile keepers say it isn't. Although the better models come equipped with thermostats, it is common for hot rocks to overheat. Owners don't discover this until the lizard's skin has been severely burned.

Safer supplemental heating elements include a specially designed heating pad that can be installed beneath the floor at one end of the tank and a ceramic heating element that provides heat but no light. Although both do the job, the heating pads have been known to crack glass enclosures. They

Some iguanas enjoy the companionship of others of their kind, but aggression may kick in when the animals reach sexual maturity.
Michael A. Siino

may also overheat, but not with the dangerous direct-contact consequences of the hot rock.

The ceramic heating element, which should be placed at the top of one end of the enclosure, is well-regarded among many experienced iguana keepers, especially those who reside in cold areas where the temperatures are very low in the winter or at night. Heralded as both safe and effective, such a heating element is preferable to leaving the incandescent heat light on and interfering with the lizard's expectations of a dark night.

Needless to say, given the specific heat requirements, an iguana's caretaker must not guess at the temperatures within the animal's habitat. These must be monitored daily by a system of thermometers, ideally positioned on the outside of each end of the enclosure. Only this way can you be sure that the inside temperature of this heat-seeking lizard's home remains within the necessary parameters.

FEEDING YOUR IGUANA

If you're looking for controversy and differences of opinion in the iguana world, talk about what to feed your iguana. While there are plenty of iguanas out there being maintained at optimum health by experienced keepers, were you to poll those individuals you would probably discover that most have divergent, and very strong, opinions on what an iguana should and should not be fed.

Chinchilla

Ferret (and Labrador Retriever)

Mantella Frog

Hedgehog

Hermit Crab

Iguana

Miniature Potbellied Pig

Ball Python

Mice

Western Tiger Salamander

Tarantula

Red-Footed Tortoise

What most agree on is that iguanas are basically vegetarians. Just how stringently they must adhere to this, however, is where the differences of opinion emerge.

We will begin with the basic vegetarian diet, composed preferably of fresh, raw fruits and vegetables. According to Phillip Samuelson, iguana enthusiast and editor of *Reptiles* magazine, this classic diet consists of about 40 percent leafy dark green vegetables (Swiss chard, dandelion greens, parsley and collard greens; avoid spinach, which can impair calcium absorption), 40 percent bulkier, pulpier types of vegetables (squashes, sweet potatoes, sprouts, carrots, green beans, etc.; try to avoid lettuce and members of the cabbage family, such as cabbage itself, cauliflower, brussels sprouts and broccoli), and 20 percent fruits and other types of foods (bananas, papayas, cantaloupe, mangos, peaches, etc.).

It is that latter 20 percent that can cause some dissension among iguana enthusiasts. Because iguanas can be prone to vitamin and mineral deficiencies, especially a dangerous deficiency of blood calcium that can lead to metabolic bone disease, some keepers believe in supplementing the diet with calcium- and protein-rich sources of animal protein. This they supply in the form of, among others, premium dry dog food (crushed for easy ingestion), scrambled eggs, cooked chicken or canned tuna.

These food items produce, among those keepers who subscribe to the classic vegetarian menu, one collective cringe. These individuals believe that animal protein will lead to health problems somewhere down the road. If you insist on feeding dog food (never cat food, which can be too rich), the vegetarian purists plead, please do so only when the animal is quite young and growing quickly, and do so sparingly. The commercial diets now available for iguanas may also be better suited to younger iguanas than they are to their elders.

Although they may not agree completely on dietary components, most keepers do concur that iguanas need variety in their diets. Chop the various foods into very small pieces (especially important for young iguanas), and then mix them all together so that an iguana with a discriminating palate cannot just pick and choose what it wants to eat at a given sitting. A good mix ensures both variety and balanced nutrition.

An example of why balance is so critical to the iguana may be seen in the relationship between the iguana, vitamin D3 and calcium. In the wild, the sunlight helps to provide the lizard with vitamin D3, which in turn assists in calcium assimilation. But in captivity, the iguana must rely on its owner and the artificial lighting, varied diet and nutritional supplements he or she provides, to receive what it needs for long-term health.

Dietary supplements can be valuable iguana-care tools, but only if they are used correctly. Ignore that all-too-human philosophy that if a little is good, more must be better. Your job is not to drown the lizard in nutrients, but rather to supplement an already healthy, well-balanced diet with a little extra calcium and vitamins. A light sprinkling of a vitamin/mineral powder formulated for reptiles on the animal's dinner once or twice a week is all it takes.

Until they reach their second birthday, young iguanas should be fed every day. After that two-year mark, every-other-day feedings should suffice. Remove uneaten food regularly to keep the enclosure sanitary, and wash food dishes after each feeding with a bleach/water mixture (rinsed off thoroughly, of course) for the same sanitation purposes.

And finally, don't forget the treats (iguana treats, not treats designed for humans!). Assuming the iguana is being fed well and receiving a proper balance of nutrients, if it is like most iguanas it will enjoy a taste of flowers from time to time. Favorite blossoms include hibiscus flowers, rose petals, carnations and geraniums, all of which must be free of pesticides or other toxins.

Salmonella and Iguanas

For several years now, we have been hearing much about the threat of salmonella, a bacterial illness that attacks humans, especially young, elderly and ill humans, with particular ferocity. What we might not hear in these reports, however, is that in addition to being transmitted by raw meat and eggs, it can also be transmitted by iguanas.

While identifying salmonella carriers, both live and inanimate, can be a challenge, incorporating simple preventive measures into our daily lives is quite simple. It works with cooking, and it can work in the keeping of pet iguanas as well. All it takes is a brief understanding of what you're dealing with.

Iguanas, and several other reptile species, such as turtles, are common carriers of this illness. Some evidence suggests that it may be more common in imported iguanas than in specimens that are bred domestically. Despite their role in salmonella transmission, however, affected lizards are not likely to exhibit any evidence of illness. While presenting the picture of health to the world and to their owners, they can transmit an illness to humans that results in severe digestive problems.

Human handlers of affected iguanas can be exposed to the bacteria by touching the animals directly, by sustaining scratches or bites from an affected iguana, by cleaning the lizard's habitat or even by touching counters or other household surfaces with which affected iguanas have come into contact. Children probably most frequently contract the disease by placing unwashed fingers in their mouths after touching affected reptiles.

Another common site of transmission can be the bathtub. One favored activity among many iguana owners is to place the lizard in a bathtub full of lukewarm water for some indoor swimming. If that iguana happens to be a salmonella carrier, and if the owner decides to take a bath after the iguana's dip, we see a natural route of salmonella transmission from reptile to human.

Of course that bathtub transmission would be easily prevented, simply by cleaning the tub thoroughly after the iguana's swimming session with an antibacterial cleaning agent.

Prevention is the name of the game for other modes of transmission, as well. To avoid contracting salmonella from an iguana, clean and disinfect the animal's cage, including branches, basking rocks and food and water dishes, as often as possible, and wash your hands thoroughly after handling the iguana or any reptiles. If you are bitten or scratched, clean the wound thoroughly with water and antibacterial soap, and treat it with an antibiotic ointment.

While hygiene is critical in the care of the iguana's habitat, so is it for your own. To prevent salmonella transmission through your own household management, store food, both yours and your iguana's, where it cannot be contaminated by reptile feces; keep iguanas away from surfaces where you prepare your family's food; and if you allow your pet to swim or soak in your bathtub or sink, clean those fixtures thoroughly afterward. If you even suspect that the iguana has come into contact with a vulnerable household surface, clean that area thoroughly with a bleach/water mixture or similarly effective antibacterial agent.

In houses where both iguanas and children younger than two years of age reside, it's usually best that the kids not handle the reptiles, as youngsters tend to be prime candidates for serious infections. For obvious reasons, this policy will probably prove beneficial for the iguanas, as well, in that they typically don't appreciate being handled by those who are rough or inexperienced.

Some who have studied the salmonella question have also suggested that it's best not to allow an iguana to run loose in the house, especially in a house where young children reside. On one hand, unsupervised freedom can be dangerous for the iguana, which, in a home that is not properly iguana-proofed, can sustain serious injury. On the other hand, the carrier iguana running freely through the house can contaminate surfaces, furniture, etc., that may then serve as conduits for the disease's transmission to family members.

You need not live in fear of salmonella, and neither must you forego choosing this stunning lizard as a pet because of the potential problems. As can be said for iguana ownership in general, and salmonella prevention in particular, practice a little common sense and institute a sound program of preventive measures, and you should all live happily ever after.

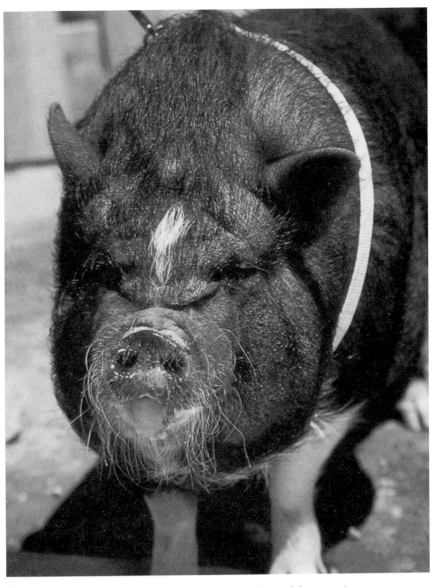

Potbellied pigs are unique pets for people who understand their requirements.
Michael A. Siino

CHAPTER 8

This Little Piggy: The Miniature Potbellied Pig

It was a dream come true—a dream come true, that is, for those whose dreams involved pigs and who likewise harbored an overpowering desire to live with them.

It was the early 1980s when the photographs began to circulate. There, in living color, perched within the arms of an adoring human, was an irresistible little character with round, shining eyes as black as obsidian; a pudgy physique and a smiling mug that cast a spell on any fortunate soul who happened to see one of the many articles written about it at the time.

WELCOME THE POTBELLIED PIG

What could be more perfect? A tiny pig you could carry comfortably in your arms, a roly-poly porcine pet no bigger than a puppy. The pig in that picture was the miniature potbellied pig, soon to be heralded as the pet of the eighties, the nineties and beyond.

Ah, but looks can be deceiving, and so can slick marketing. Those delightful pig pictures motivated people to seek out pig pets in droves. What they found indeed met all their expectations: small pigs that could be held comfortably in their arms, charmers in every sense of the word.

But what was not so widely publicized, and what soon became apparent to owners nationwide, was the fact that those diminutive animals featured so

The Miniature Potbellied Pig as a Pet

	Light	1	2	3	4	5	Heavy
TIME COMMITMENT						🐖	
MAINTENANCE Grooming					🐖		
Feeding					🐖		
General Clean-Up						🐖	
SUITABILITY TO CHILDREN Ages Infant-5	🐖						
Ages 5-10			🐖				
Over 10			🐖				
SOCIABILITY						🐖	
EXPENSE OF KEEPING						🐖	

adorably in all those photographs, in all those marketing materials, were pig*lets*, not full-grown pigs. The delight of those impulsive pig buyers turned to dismay as they watched their pets gradually tip the scales at forty pounds, fifty pounds, sixty pounds, seventy—some even reaching the ninety-pound mark or more.

What these owners misunderstood, aside from the need to learn such facts ahead of time, was the word "miniature" in their pets' name. Yes, these are miniature pigs when one considers them within the context of pigs and hogs at large, but they apparently were not miniature in the context of many an ignorant owner's expectations of the word. And, unfortunately, many pig sellers at the time were none too anxious to clarify the misunderstandings of the potential pig-buying public.

THE RISE—AND FALL—OF THE POTBELLIED PIG

And so this episode in pig history simply heaped more fuel on the already maligned reputation of the pig family at large, a reputation based on false though universally accepted claims regarding porcine character and habits.

You know the drill. Pigs are dirty. Pigs are nasty. Pigs are dim-witted. All pigs care to do is eat like gluttons and wallow in the mud.

While many enchanted would-be pig owners were willing to cast aside these impressions at the first sight of those adorable, so-called miniature pigs, they gladly reclaimed them as gospel when it appeared the relationship just wouldn't work out. What really happened was that their own inabilities to care for their pets properly led to an epidemic of aggressive, mean-spirited pigs wallowing in the mud.

At the same time, there were other owners for whom the moment of truth spelled heartbreak. They had bonded deeply with their pets, which, as those who know the species can attest, is a phenomenon frequently inspired by pigs of all sizes. Yet they realized they would not be able to offer these animals the kind of life they required. Despite their deep affections for their pigs, they had to give them up, the dream of that initial inspiration shattered, the promise betrayed.

Which leaves us today not with a trendy pet that stands ready to take the pet world by storm, but a pet whose popularity fire, fortunately, has been dampened somewhat. While miniature potbellied pigs are still ending up in the wrong hands from time to time—and thus still being sent off to animal shelters and special sanctuaries founded specifically for the care of discarded

Some pig sellers may claim the animals only grow to 40 or 50 pounds, but the truth is miniature potbellies can reach 90 to 100 pounds. *Michael A. Siino*

pig pets—the orbit in which these animals move today is quite a bit brighter, and looking better all the time.

GETTING TO KNOW THE MISUNDERSTOOD PIG

There is nothing more adorable than a piglet. Round. Soft-furred. Cuddly. But soon this potbellied piglet will grow into a much larger, more demanding, and to some, even frightening creature. The soft piglet fur makes way for a bristly coat sprouted from thick, even scaly looking skin. Tusks sprout from beneath the pig's upper lip, and that demanding nature that was so manageable when the pig was young is no longer funny when the spoiled piglet becomes an adult.

Another surprise to many newcomers to the world of pigs is the fact that pigs in general are extremely intelligent animals, the potbellied variety being no exception. They are frequently said to be more intelligent than dogs, and, say some owners, more intelligent than a lot of people you may know. With such smarts at their disposal, they have proven to be quite manipulative within their households, adept at training their owners to bend to their every will.

The potbellied pig's often headstrong intelligence will become most obvious when the animal reaches about one-and-a-half to two years of age. At this time, assuming its behavior has never been directed in more positive directions or been drawn boundaries, the pig may become aggressive and challenge its owners for leadership in the household. This is especially true if the animal has been kept indoors as a housepet, allowed to run herd over the family since piglethood. It can become destructive and even quite territorial; its home is its castle and, thus, its territory.

It's not surprising to see pigs newly arrived at this level of maturity directed to local animal shelters by owners who don't know what to do. They didn't know how to recognize, let alone control, their pets' potentially damaging characteristics when the pigs were young, and they have no idea how to deal with the problem now.

A pig's natural rooting behavior can also be a problem for improperly prepared owners, especially when those owners attempt to keep these animals in suburban areas where such behavior is unacceptable. Give a potbellied pig the run of an expensively landscaped backyard, for example, and that yard will soon look like a mine field. For owners not truly dedicated to pig keeping, if faced with the choice between a yard and a pig, the pig is not likely to emerge victorious.

But, of course, rooting behavior is as natural to a pig as breathing, and simply something would-be owners must be willing to accept and to

Pigs are natural rooters who enjoy the outdoors; unprepared owners will find their lawns turned to mine fields without forethought and planning. *Michael A. Siino*

accommodate. They must do the same in regard to the pig's eventual size, which typically ranges between fifty to ninety pounds at adulthood. Whether talking size, living space or behavior, prepare yourself for the truths about these pigs before taking the plunge into pig keeping, and prevent surprises— and heartbreaks—later on.

Despite how it may have been marketed in the past, this is not the ideal pet for every family. Through the years, far too many owners who succumbed to both the hype and to the pig's charms, have had to give their pigs up simply because the animals grew too big or too difficult to handle. Rather than preparing themselves for pig ownership, they learned the hard way that this just wasn't the right pet path for them, and the pig became the byproduct of that mistake.

Stories abound of heartbroken owners, callous owners, overfed pigs, underfed pigs, abandoned pigs, injured pigs—all victims of ignorant owners. But that need not be the case today. With the immense economic rewards of breeding potbellied pigs now a thing of the past, these animals have a better chance of landing in homes where they truly belong, and, thus, of enjoying a brighter future.

WHAT MAKES A POTBELLIED PIG SO SPECIAL

For those who do understand pigs and refuse to underestimate the commitment required for these animals' care, there is no better pet. Such individuals cannot for a moment stop singing the praises of the miniature potbellied pig. On this brighter side, we find a wonderfully inquisitive animal who, with proper handling and molding, can be a terrific companion and a heck of a lot of fun. Most can even be housebroken.

Owners who share this particular pet obsession are especially enamored of the pigs' intelligence and flattered by the animals' demands for social interactions with and attention from their families. This mutual admiration can spawn a deep bond between pig and owner. A bond that, thanks to the unique soul of the potbellied pig, can even develop within a not-so-perfect relationship. This, of course, only compounds the devastation when an ill-prepared owner must give up this animal for logistical reasons.

The brighter future of the potbellied pig has much to do with the nature of the pig owners and breeders themselves these days. While the pigs are now attracting more prepared, knowledgeable owners, which of course only benefits the animals in their care, pig ownership itself is becoming quite a bit friendlier for those owners, as well.

One example of this is price. In the 1980s, potbellied pig prices soared along with the pigs' popularity, even though that popularity had a rather shaky foundation based on less-than-accurate facts. As usually happens with such phenomena, potbellied pig breeding attracted a great many disreputable breeders and promoters. Most of those breeders have now, thankfully, dropped by the wayside for lack of profits, leaving the innocent fruits of their entrepreneurial endeavors to those who place pig well-being above profits.

Would-be pig owners now have a larger pool of good breeders to whom to turn when seeking a potbellied pig pet. Such breeders love the pigs, and they share an overriding passion to spread information that is correct and true about the pigs' care and character. They want only those who share their own deep passions for these unique animals to buy them and make them lifelong members of the family.

This does not mean that potential pig owners should let down their guard and ignore the need to gather knowledge about these animals. They must still be savvy about what they are looking for. (In fact, some unethical breeders have even been known to sell large agricultural-breed pigs to uninformed owners who learned too late that their new pets were not of the potbellied variety after all.) Intelligent, clear-headed screening of breeders remains paramount, even when you find yourself falling madly in love with the rotund little bundle of piglet cuddled into your arms, snuffling affectionately into your ear.

But even before you reach this point, no matter how well-informed you may be about the care of the potbellied pig, no matter how reputable the breeder before you seems to be, you must first honestly evaluate your own living situation to ensure it can accommodate, both physically and legally, an animal of this type.

IS THIS THE PET FOR YOU?

Although it can spend time indoors with its family and enjoy those times immensely, the potbellied pig is not an appropriate pet choice for apartment or condominium dwellers. It needs an outdoor enclosure in which it may spend at least part of its time. Furthermore, zoning restrictions in some areas prohibit the keeping of so-called farm animals in residential areas. In some of these areas, the potbellied pig, even though bred solely to be a pet, may be considered a farm animal.

In some states, owners may be allowed to keep potbellied pigs but are required to obtain a state health certificate because their pets are categorized technically as livestock animals. Look into this. Investigate all possible obstacles that could crop up later. That is certainly preferable to living in ignorance with a very bondable pet that you suddenly discover you are no longer allowed to keep.

Some breeders further believe that potbellied pigs do best in homes without children. These sensitive, intelligent critters that are so easily spoiled may come to view themselves as equal to the kids, and thus become aggressive toward the human youngsters if they believe they are not receiving equal treatment. You may work around this potential obstacle by raising a young pig with the kids, teaching all to live and work together. With gentle yet firm handling, help the young pig to understand its place and its boundaries within the family. This latter activity is in fact critical in any pig household, those with kids and those without.

There seems to be no overall preference on which gender makes the better pet. As with most species in this book, spaying and neutering play a role, but all in all, some owners just naturally prefer females to males and vice versa. Neither gender is messier; either can approach mealtime and playtime with great gusto, and owners must simply be prepared for the inevitable results.

FINDING YOUR POTBELLIED PIG

Once the decks are cleared on the preliminaries and you have deemed your home and your family as ideal for pig ownership, you may begin the search for the perfect potbellied pet.

Before you buy a pig, try to visit one in its natural environment where it was born and raised. *Michael A. Siino*

The best pet pig candidate is an animal that is housebroken, well-socialized, spayed or neutered, trained to walk on a leash, vaccinated and fond of humans. A breeder offering such a pig is more likely to be one you can trust. If this breeder further insists (and backs this up in writing) that you return the pig to him or her should things between you and your pet not work out, you know you are dealing with someone who truly cares about the fate of the animals he or she breeds.

Purchasing from a breeder enables you to see where the pig was bred and spent those first formative weeks, as you will probably have to visit the facility to choose and get to know your pig. This also allows you to observe the pig in a more natural environment where you need not make such excuses as "He's only acting like that because this is a strange environment and he's stressed." He shouldn't be stressed on his home turf, and if he is healthy and well-socialized, there is no reason he should be anything but a contented, friendly piglet.

You should also try to meet the piglet's parents and siblings, especially its mother. Watch it interact with the other pigs and with the people who bred and care for it. This will tell you much about the breeders as well as the pig. When evaluating a pet of such intelligence and social nature, observations of how it behaves with other pigs and with humans are critical.

You will notice that there is no mention here of evaluating a pet store as a potential source of a pet potbellied pig. While these animals are often offered through pet stores, displayed prominently and irresistibly in pens at the front of their stores, even in shopping malls in the most urban of areas, this is not the best place to purchase potbellied pigs. The animals may not be as healthy and well-socialized as those offered by private breeders, and the sellers may not be all that concerned with whether the pig is right for you, or whether you are right for the pig.

A good breeder will probably speak endlessly about care and behavior and want to know all he or she possibly can about your own living situation and how that might affect the pig. Do you travel a lot? How many hours a day is someone at home? Do you have an enclosed yard?

Dealing this way with a breeder, you—and the pig—are far less likely to fall into the trap of the impulse buy. A good breeder is genuinely concerned about the long-term well-being of his or her pigs. Isn't this the type of person you would like involved when you are considering a pet, and a commitment, such as this?

What to Look For in Your Pig

When screening breeders, beware of those who seem fixated on the small size of the pigs he or she either breeds or would like to breed. Some place too much importance on this, and while small pigs are delightful, they may not have the bone required to support the weight of the animal's body. Such an animal may suffer leg problems and be forced to drag the large belly from which it takes its name on the ground. What you should look for in a pet potbellied pig is overall health and consistent structure, thus ensuring the pig's bones are healthy and strong and compatible with the overall size of the pig. A healthy conformation helps to ensure a longer, more comfortable life for the pig—and fewer veterinarian bills for you.

Other than that, choose a pig with bright, clear eyes. Make sure the animal's skin is free of rashes and that the pig does not seem to scratch excessively. The pig should be lively, friendly and curious (depression or lethargy are signs of trouble in a vivacious animal such as this). And, of course, the pig should be plump. Not so plump, mind you, that its belly drags on the ground or that it seems to have difficulty moving, but a healthy-looking plump commensurate with a healthy pig.

UNEXPECTED SURPRISES IN THE POTBELLIED PIG

While some might consider it a face only a mother could love, to those who have found themselves enamored of the potbellied pig, this animal's mug is a face that can't help but make you smile. That is how those who have come to know the potbellied pig most readily describe this rather unlikely pet. Whether black, white, silver or a combination of these, once you see a potbellied pig with its shining eyes, swayed back, signature pot belly and pencil-like tail that wags furiously and constantly, you are not likely to soon forget it.

What may come as most surprising when meeting a passel of potbellied pigs is how really very quiet they are, so unlike the more common image of pigs emoting ear-splitting squeals and guttural grunts. What you are most likely to hear are the soft grunts and purrs of the happy, contented pig, which we would hope is the pig's frame of mind most of the time. This is not to say that this animal's vocabulary does not also include its share of squeals, though those are usually reserved for those moments when the pig is calling for dinner or when it is frightened. These moments can be corrected, if not altogether prevented.

During that first meeting, you are also likely to notice that constantly wagging tail. It's voice-activated, some say. Speak and it starts up like a windmill in a hurricane. Stop speaking, and the tail stops too.

Do not, however, automatically assume that that wagging tail is an invitation on the part of the pig to be picked up in the arms of a human. The level and nature of handling is a personal issue among pigs. Some truly enjoy that type of intimacy, while for others, being held takes them back instinctively to their wild past when the only time they were lifted into the air was by predators. Of course most become too large to be held comfortably anyway, but be sensitive to your pet's way of seeing the world and treat it with only the utmost gentleness and kindness (tempered, as we will see, with firmness).

SPOILED AND SELFISH

A picture of a most friendly pig is what we have drawn here, but do not be mistaken. One of the first messages the fledgling owner of a potbellied pig must embrace is the fact that there are few pets as easily spoiled as this irresistible pig. Live with this intelligent, even manipulative animal for a few weeks or even days, and you will see clearly how this comes to be. Before its owners even realize what is happening, the pig casts its spell, leaving the owner to wonder just how this was allowed to happen.

The spoiling of a pig and the consequences of that pig's behavior are no laughing matter. A spoiled pig, one whose every whim is granted, whether that means napping on the antique couch in the living room or demanding it be served its owner's ice cream cone, is a pig prone to destructive behavior, aggression, intense separation anxiety—and a one-way ticket to the animal shelter.

Your pig has to learn to respect your wishes. Training works best if there's a suitable reward—like a treat—for doing something. *Michael A. Siino*

Instead, from the very beginning, channel this animal's energy and intelligence in a more positive direction. As intelligent and, therefore, opinionated as they can be, potbellied pigs thrive with training, especially training grounded in positive reinforcement, ideally with treat rewards.

While their intellect is often compared to that of the dog, which, for the most part, is driven to please its owner, the priority of the potbellied pig, say those who know it best, is to please itself (thus perhaps making it more like humans than like dogs).

This motivation begins as soon as the pigs begin to navigate in the big world around them at just a few weeks of age. They learn to express their desires and to manipulate, which explains just why those cute little round piglets are so easy to spoil. But such behavior is no longer cute when that piglet matures into a very headstrong seventy-pound adult who has become accustomed to having every wish granted with just a single squeal or a stare at its owner.

It is your job as owner, a role you must not forget, to set down the rules and boundaries early for this animal. Do this not with physical punishment, but with preemptive measures just as we try to do in managing the young of our own species. You do not wait until a child becomes a teenager to begin to enforce rules, and the same applies to the management of a pig. If the pig will not be allowed on the couch as an adult, it should not be allowed on the couch as a piglet. If the pig will not be allowed to sleep in your bedroom as an adult, it should not be allowed to sleep there as a piglet. You get the picture.

Of course one way to get these messages across in a positive manner is with clear, consistent commands and those treat rewards we talked about. As most owners have realized, you must give a potbellied pig a good reason to obey your whims rather than its own, and a favored treat is usually the appropriate tool for doing this.

HOUSETRAINING YOUR PIG

You must use this same positive reinforcement in housetraining the pig. Yes, housetraining. Despite the reputation of pigs as animals that are happiest when burrowed in filth (another untruth that plagues them), pigs prefer cleanliness, and, if possible, they prefer to perform their bathroom duties in a single spot. Housetrain a potbellied pig as you would a dog not by "rubbing the animal's nose in it" (an unfortunate untruth that plagues the dog), but by communicating your expectations to the pig clearly and rewarding it for complying.

While pigs can and have been trained to use a litter box in the house (indoor litter boxes should be filled with pine shavings, no cedar), the preferred, most convenient, method—and one that reduces indoor odors—is to train them to use a designated spot outdoors and to establish a pattern there. Take the pig to this spot several times during the day, especially after meals or when it seems to be exhibiting the restless signs of impending elimination, and even give it a command, such as "potty," so it can learn to associate a command with this activity. When it eliminates in this area, praise it profusely and offer it a treat as a reward.

If you aren't able to get the pig to this area on time or you fail to read the signs—and there will be plenty of those times during the housetraining process—try to catch the pig in the act and get it to the appropriate spot immediately so it can make a mental connection between the act and the spot. If, on the other hand, you do not catch it in the act and you find the evidence of an accident in the house, don't bother scolding the animal. The moment is gone. You must simply wait until the next time when you can again apply those more positive techniques.

KEEPING YOUR POTBELLIED PIG HEALTHY

The healthy potbellied pig can live as long as twenty years. The key word here, of course, being "healthy."

The challenge of fostering health and longevity in a potbellied pig is allayed with a simple commitment to commonsense handling. This, of course, involves finding a veterinarian skilled in the care of these animals and following a few simple guidelines with his or her assistance.

First, preventive medicine. Periodic visits to the vet will help ensure that the tusks are not impairing the pig's ability to eat, that the skin and hair are healthy, that the animal's weight is on target, that the pig is suffering no foot or joint problems and that generally all is well.

The vaccinations that a pet potbellied pig should receive depend on the area of the country in which it lives, as well as the other animals (and the other pigs) with which it will be in contact. Here the veterinarian's advice will be valuable as he or she will be familiar with the types of pig-prone illnesses native to the pig's environment, and what vaccines are available to protect the pig. While some such vaccines are mandated by local public health policies, which may, for example, recommend that potbellied pigs be vaccinated against rabies, other vaccines are best ordered by the pig's veterinarian.

Deworming is another important preventive measure for keeping the pig healthy. This should be done first when the pig is seven weeks old, again at nine to eleven weeks of age, and from then on whenever necessary or as recommended by the veterinarian. Pay close attention to the pig's feces for signs of worms that can appear there, as well as for any changes, such as sudden diarrhea, that can be strong indicators of internal problems brewing within.

Spaying and neutering are also important pig issues, the consensus being that every pet potbellied pig should be spayed or neutered. This is especially true of males, which can make wonderful pets if neutered, but are far too aggressive if left intact.

Spaying and neutering help prevent the birth of unwanted piglets in an environment already plagued by the existence of too many unwanted pigs, but it also makes for better pig pets. While neutering does help reduce odor in male pigs and helps them to become more acceptable pets than they would otherwise be, altering in general is a positive step toward viewing these pigs as pets rather than breeders.

An altered pig, when handled with firm and gentle consistency, is a better companion, content to focus more on its family's activities than on the gender and behavior of other pigs. In most cases, then, the pig's temperament will be superior to that of an intact animal. You must, however, find a veterinarian to perform this procedure who is experienced in working with and anesthetizing pigs. The breeder should be able to recommend someone and probably will before you even think to ask.

Despite the typical image of pigs as dirty and wallowing in the mud, odor is something that rarely plagues the pet potbellied pig, assuming of course that the males are neutered. The only time a bath may be necessary is if the pig is going to be participating in a potbellied pig show, and even then, the bath could prove to be more stressful for the pig than the show itself.

Some special attention may be required to the pig's skin, hooves and tusks, the most common potential problem being dryness. There are special products, such as moisturizers and conditioners, now on the market designed especially for pigs to alleviate this. If dryness proves to be a problem with your pig, you can also try supplementing its diet with an occasional spoonful of oil about once a week or so, which can help prevent the problem from the inside out.

Pigs are actually quite similar to humans physically and even mentally. Think of the type of living situations in which you yourself thrive best and apply those tenets to the care of your pig. They, like us, can be headstrong and opinionated in behavior. They, like us, can be prone to such respiratory ailments as pneumonia, so they must not be situated in an environment, either indoor or outdoor, that is too hot or too cold. All in all, potbellied pigs need access to sunshine and shade, fresh air, mentally stimulating activity, good food, a clean environment and lots of attention from those they love—just like we do.

A HOUSE NO WOLF CAN BLOW DOWN

We've all heard about the three little pigs and the two who had their homes blown down by the big bad wolf. Of course the destruction was directly linked to the fact that those homes, one of straw, one of wood, were thrown together haphazardly by two little pigs who were more interested in play than in work. The owner of the potbellied pig is thus wiser to follow the example of the third little pig, who sacrificed leisure hours in favor of carefully constructing an indestructible house of bricks.

Despite the original hype that led the public to believe the potbellied pig was the consummate housepet, for most, the primary home is usually outdoors. Many pet potbellied pigs do spend a great deal of time indoors with their families, yet even the pig who enjoys indoor living requires a home of its own outdoors. All pigs thrive best if afforded some time out and about in the fresh air and sunshine.

Fortunately, you need not hire a brick mason to construct this animal's outdoor digs. Several alternatives are available that will not be toppled easily. A simple doghouse, made of either wood or heavy plastic, is a good, solid

A wooden doghouse can serve the same purposes—to provide shelter and shade—for your potbellied pig.
Michael A. Siino

outdoor structure. The plastic models are easy and flexible to position, and even easier to clean.

The house should be elevated up off the ground to prevent chills and moisture from seeping in. So should the floor of the house be lined with bedding material of hay, straw or old blankets. (Blankets are more appropriate for females than for males because males may become too aggressive and destructive with the blankets.) The pigs love to nest and burrow into the hay bedding, and some pigs have even been known to enjoy wrapping themselves up in the blankets.

In addition, the house should be surrounded by a well-constructed pig-proof enclosure that will, while allowing the pig room to stretch and enjoy the great outdoors, keep the animal confined, especially when it is not being supervised by its owner. The enclosure should be situated in the yard so that the pig has access to both sunshine and shade. Shade is very important, as it protects the pig from sunburn, a common condition in the pig exposed to direct sunlight.

While bedding material is an essential component inside the house, it is also a critical element for the floor of the enclosure at large. Clean pine shavings, straw or hay will, on one hand, prevent this hoofed animal from sliding around and possibly sustaining injury on slippery ground, and, on the other, provide it with a medium in which it can joyfully burrow and root.

Above all, you are seeking to cushion and protect the pig from coming into direct contact with concrete or other potentially hard, cold surfaces, which have been accused of causing joint problems in potbellied pigs. As a final act, place a litter box in the pen filled with pine shavings (no cedar), and you have created an outdoor enclosure fit for a porcine king.

A CLEAN CREATURE BY NATURE

The potbellied pig harbors a natural affinity for its own cleanliness, an affinity it extends to the condition of its habitat and the bedding within its house, as well. Forget the image of the pig wallowing in the mud and reveling in filth. For a potbellied pig, cleanliness is next to pigliness.

Placing a litter box filled with pine shavings in the enclosure will help you keep your pig's home clean, but with or without the box, you must remove feces and soiled bedding regularly to prevent an unhappy pig.

As a final amenity, consider providing the animal with a water source for soaking. While some owners have provided their pets with a mud puddle to wade around in, when given the choice these pigs will usually choose water over mud. The pig can instead wallow quite nicely in a child's wading pool filled with water. Within this pool, the animal can cool itself off and keep clean at the same time. Be warned, however, that the feel of the water may stimulate the pig to use the water as a bathroom.

A DIET FIT FOR A PIG

If there is one element of the pig's universal reputation that can be considered true, that would probably have to be the animal's love of food. What is false in this image, however, is that it is appropriate to feed the potbellied pig scraps and garbage, that it will thrive on virtually anything you choose to give it.

While a food-loving pig might try and convince you otherwise, it, like any pet, requires a high-quality diet to keep it plump and healthy—but not too plump, a condition that will undermine its health. Obviously the potbellied pig is prone to obesity, signs of which include impaired movement, back problems, and a pot belly that is too rotund and hangs too low to the ground. Potbellied pigs do love to eat, evident in the success owners reap in using treat rewards as a training tool. Yet the downside of this obsession is that

Potbellied pigs eat and drink with gusto, so be prepared for the cleanup involved in the aftermath.
Michael A. Siino

their persistent personalities also succeed in coercing owners to overfeed them. Resist that temptation.

Like the ideal diet of their owners, the potbellied pig's diet should be high in fiber and low in fat, fed in conjunction with a constant supply of fresh, clean water. The pig's nutritional needs should be met with a diet not of table scraps and garbage, but one composed primarily of pelleted commercial pig chow formulated specifically for miniature pigs. Several brands of this type of feed are now available at feed stores and large pet supply stores. Store the chow in airtight containers that will keep it fresh and protect it from mice and mold.

Most owners feed their pigs twice a day—out of clean food dishes, of course—and supplement this with vegetables, fruit, grasses, hay and alfalfa, perhaps a sliced apple every morning with breakfast, and fruits and vegetables as treats. It's as easy as that.

Some time outdoors grazing in the yard (on pesticide-free vegetation) also provides a healthy supplement and an interesting nutrition-related activity for the pig. One far more constructive than allowing this food monger to clean the leftovers off the dinner plates or mooch a piece of chocolate birthday cake. If you don't have a yard where your pig can graze, you can supplement the pig's diet with timothy hay, which will satisfy the animal's need to munch without adding too much protein to the pig's diet.

GETTING ACTIVE WITH YOUR PIG

Potbellied pigs crave activity, especially when this means spending some quality time with their owners. This certainly is not a pet that can be left alone for long periods of time (or for some particularly spoiled individuals, even short periods of time). Separation anxiety can be a problem with these pigs, a problem that may be eased somewhat with activity and exercise, which will also benefit the pig's overall health.

Some pigs like toys such as large, swallow-resistant balls and squeaky dog toys they can push around and nuzzle with their snouts. Training sessions or simply burrowing into pine shavings or hay bedding can even be seen as games as they are favored activities for so many pigs.

The same may be said for walks on a leash, an activity that will feed this animal's insatiable curiosity, introduce it to new sights and sounds beyond its

Special harnesses designed specifically for potbellied pigs can make walking one of these unique creatures almost as simple as walking a dog—assuming, of course, that the pig is amenable.
Michael A. Siino

familiar territory and extend the socialization process into new environs. Use an H-shaped harness for your pig's leash, introduce this concept to the animal gently and gradually as early as possible and, as always, have those rewards handy. All in all, be patient. If yours is a pig that simply is not interested in this activity, evident in a failure to make any progress in eliciting its acceptance of it, respect that too. Don't force it.

Potbellied pigs should, as a rule, get along with other pets in the household because they are such social creatures. Success in this area depends on how the pig is socialized. As mentioned elsewhere in this chapter, potbellied pigs can be easily spoiled. Though a pig's demands may seem cute when the animal is young, they can turn downright nasty when the pig weighs close to a hundred pounds and has no concept of the word "compromise." It may take its spoiled behavior out on everyone else in the family—whether they be human, canine, feline or porcine.

As for the pig who does enjoy showing off away from home, who has proven itself to be wonderfully socialized to other people and even other animals, who has become, if you'll pardon the expression, the quintessential ham, that pig may be an ideal candidate for the show ring.

Today potbellied pigs can be registered with potbellied pig associations that work to standardize breeding and promote proper care and ownership. These associations, as well as state and local fairs, often sponsor potbellied pig shows, featuring these animals in a variety of classes from championship classes to the waggiest tail to trick classes. There are even costume classes, in which the most easygoing, patient of pigs allow themselves to be paraded around in every type of costume imaginable.

While such activities may sound silly to the uninitiated, they can be genuine fun for people who share a profound passion for the potbellied pig. They also serve dual duty, providing avenues for some very positive porcine experiences and training.

Showing helps reduce territorial behavior in potbellied pigs by helping the animals learn to adjust well to new surroundings, new people and new pigs; it can even help prevent separation anxiety once the pig has returned home to the old routine; and it can keep stress in check, a definite benefit as stress can be extremely debilitating, and even fatal, for these very sensitive animals.

What you will soon realize when you take the plunge into organized activity with pigs is that, while showing provides such a multitude of beneficial services to the pig, at the same time it brings people together who have come under the spell of this demanding, though fascinating, pet species. These people indeed share a passion unique within the world at large and usually enjoy meeting others of their same mindsets. Coming together in that way, comparing care notes and oohing and aahing over other pigs, just adds to the fun of living with potbellied pigs.

Rats make friendly, intelligent pets that enjoy human interactions and can't resist an occasional sightseeing tour on an owner's shoulder. *Michael A. Siino*

CHAPTER 9

Split Personality: The Rat and Mouse

Eeek! The terrified woman shrieks, leaps onto the seat of the nearest chair and refuses to come down until the animal that just scampered across the kitchen is destroyed.

Hmmm. Now consider the animal that has elicited this violent reaction. It's an inch, maybe two in length (not counting its tail), it weighs all of one ounce, it has a tiny wiggling nose, small rounded ears and a soft silky coat of gray fur. It is also ten times more frightened at this moment than the ridiculous creature screaming down at it from the chair.

This diminutive, and no doubt extremely confused, creature is, of course, the mouse.

What mixed messages we have sent this tiny animal through the years. First, we have Mickey, the tuxedoed rodent who plays host at the world's most famous theme park, not to mention featured roles in books, cartoons and films. We then find countless other mice serving as inspirations to artists, makers of stuffed animals, cartoonists and greeting card designers worldwide. But spot a real mouse, the genuine article, in the kitchen, and pandemonium breaks loose. How ridiculous it makes us seem.

But of course not all humans are terrified of mice, or of its larger, even more maligned cousin, the rat. These are individuals who have discovered the secret: that mice, and yes, rats too, can make wonderful pets when we invite them into our homes. Open your mind to the possibility, and you may be surprised at what you'll find.

Rats and Mice as Pets

	Light	1	2	3	4	5	Heavy
TIME COMMITMENT				🐀			
MAINTENANCE Grooming			🐀				
Feeding				🐀			
General Clean-Up				🐀			
SUITABILITY TO CHILDREN Ages Infant-5		🐀					
Ages 5-10				🐀			
Over 10						🐀	
SOCIABILITY					🐀		
EXPENSE OF KEEPING				🐀			

"VERMIN" AS PETS

Although it is quite a large and rather variegated family, when most of us hear the word rodent we immediately think of rats and mice. It's a word not typically used in a positive vein, and one most often associated when the subject is pestilence.

The word rodent actually comes from the Latin verb *rodere*, meaning to gnaw, an activity in which every rodent partakes. A rodent's teeth are engineered ideally for gnawing, and they continue growing throughout the animal's life. While it may choose an external object to gnaw, say a block of wood or a cardboard cereal box, if its jaws and teeth are properly structured, the mouse or rat will grind its teeth together to keep them trim and sharp.

Of course most humans who have considered themselves terrorized by these creatures in their homes are typically more concerned with eradication than they are with rodent dental health. As a result, rats and mice, both pets and those that live wild, have gotten a bad rap. We don't want the wild ones in our food supplies, and we don't want them living in or around our homes—and for good reason. Wild rats and mice can carry disease and parasites; it was rats that were responsible for the Black Plague in medieval Europe. Of course the true transmitters of that devastating plague epidemic were the fleas that had chosen rats as their hosts, not the rats themselves, but that fact often gets lost in the telling.

Today, while the threat of plague and other potential rodent-borne disease is minimal, it's not a good idea to live with wild mice or rats, or to invite them into our homes. Don't panic. Simply store foods, including pet foods and bird seed, securely in airtight, rodent-proof containers, and you remove an important enticement to an opportunistic rat or mouse seeking a free meal.

Their unacceptable wild cousins, should, however, in no way detract from the domestic rat's or mouse's pet potential. Just make sure to heed the key word here: "domestic." Although rats and mice can make fine pets, they must never be taken from the wild. In addition to being potential carriers of disease and parasites, wild rats and mice are understandably more aggressive than their domestic cousins, their sole goal in captivity being to escape; hardly the characteristics of an ideal pet.

Mice and rats have been domesticated for many thousands of years. At the same time, the wild members of their species played key roles in the domestication of the cat, who was recruited for natural rodent population control. Together, these rodents have occupied a niche of one kind or another close to human existence throughout most of our species' history, the wild ones actually enjoying an almost symbiotic relationship with us. Where people are, these animals learned a long, long time ago, there is food. And lots of it. So follow the people and you'll never be hungry.

Of the two, mice have historically been seen in the more positive light. With their diminutive size, feather-soft fur and tiny ears, they are undeniably cute. They have even been cast as gods in some cultures. While we prefer

More nervous and skittish than rats, mice tend to be less amenable to handling and are usually more content left within the security of their habitat. *Michael A. Siino*

that wild mice remain out in the field where they belong, even that terrified woman on the chair might venture to ooh and ahh a bit upon spotting a tiny mouse nosing through the garden. But most of us would go absolutely ballistic at the thought of a rat in the house, or anywhere near our property for that matter.

Because of the rat's reputation, people are typically more inclined to accept the keeping of mice as pets than they are of rats. Take some time to look beyond society's traditional reactions, and you will see what amazing, resilient creatures rats have been since the dawn of recorded history.

Hardy, intelligent beings with breeding rates as staggering as those of the mouse, rats have successfully survived just about everything human and natural history could throw their way. Shipwrecks, fires, floods, pestilence, exterminator companies, none can phase the rat. It's a safe bet that rats, with that relentless survival instinct and accompanying savvy personality, will continue to thrive long after we are gone.

RAT OR MOUSE: WHICH WAY TO GO?

Today, in a world where the keeping of pets is becoming more and more restrictive due to time restraints and "no pets" residence policies, domestic rats and mice can fill a deep-seated void for someone who wants a pet but who is limited by space, time or a "no pets" clause in a rental agreement. Mice and rats are quiet, they require very little space and they are quite easy keepers.

Some people prefer mice to rats and vice versa. It all depends on the type of pet you are looking for.

Mice are some of the tiniest pets you may have. They weigh almost nothing, and they are very adaptable, alert and fun to watch. In fact, many equate the keeping of mice with the keeping of fish in an aquarium. Keep several together in a large habitat, and they can provide hours of relaxing observation.

Given their small size, mice are understandably timid and require owners who are sensitive to their outlook on life. They rely on a keen sense of smell and hearing to perceive the world around them, yet they are easily frightened. They are fastidious animals that are constantly grooming themselves and each other. While females emit almost no odor, the urine of males can be quite strong, thus signaling the need for cage cleaning to keep the odor in check.

While mice can be easy on the eye, many pet owners consider rats to be better pets for people seeking an animal that is interactive and affectionate with its owners. Rats are quite a bit larger than mice, and much smarter than mice (they may even be smarter than some people you know).

We use the word "rat" to describe disreputable individuals, but given the fact that rats are actually very much like people, perhaps we should use the

Mice and rats are extremely social critters that are happiest when housed with others of their kind—but keep genders together to prevent a rodent population explosion! *Michael A. Siino*

term to describe people as a whole. Rats are generally very people-oriented. They have, after all, lived on the periphery of human existence for thousands of years and have thus learned there can be great rewards from a close association with humans.

Described by veteran rat keepers as "busy bodies," rats can be delightful, interactive companions. Approach the cage and you may be greeted by a wiggling nose, bright eyes and the exuberance of a rodent just begging to come out and play. If the room is properly rat-proofed to protect furnishings and rat alike, rats can spend supervised time outside the cage and have a grand old time with their owners.

A fun-loving, curious rat, with the help of treat rewards, can be taught to come when you call its name or make kissy sounds, and some can even learn tricks. Depending on their particular personalities, they have been known to follow family members around the house like dogs, and brazenly insinuate themselves into household games and activities. Or the rat might prefer to remain perched on a trusted family member's shoulder—many a pet rat's favorite observation deck—content to remain there watching the world and nibbling on a nearby ear. When naptime comes around, it may then travel down to your lap for a snooze while you sit and watch television.

Living with mice and rats can be more enjoyable than one might imagine, perhaps even too enjoyable when we consider the major drawback in keeping them: their short lifespans.

Typically rats live about two to three years, mice a bit less. While improvements in care seem to be lengthening this average, this is still a short existence. What may ease the grief of losing a favorite is keeping more than one (rats with rats, mice with mice; don't mix the two). This will not only please these very social animals, but will help make losing one easier on the owner when that inevitable time comes.

SELECTING A RODENT PET

Although it may not live as long as we would like, choosing a pet rat or mouse with care can help ensure it will remain with you for as long as possible. The most common source of pet rats and mice is a pet shop, but you may also discover breeders in your area who produce special types of mice and rats. Pets from breeders may be more expensive, but according to the old tenet about getting what you pay for, you may be getting a healthier, better socialized animal in the long run.

Today rats and mice are found in a variety of colors, and are even bred in "fancy" varieties by fanciers who exhibit them in shows. At shows the mice and rats are judged on their colors and markings as well as on their tractable temperaments. While shows serve as good public relations venues for animals that are in need of some good press, they also can help bring lovers of rats and mice in contact with others who have discovered the charm and addictive nature of living with these animals.

Purchasing rats and mice from a trustworthy source not only ups the odds that the animals will be healthy, but also that you'll know exactly what you're getting in terms of gender. It's nice to know if you are purchasing more than one that you are indeed receiving the two males or the two females you asked for. That is certainly preferable to finding out three weeks later with the arrival of a large litter of micelets or ratlets that Fred and Barney were actually Fred and Wilma.

When evaluating prospective new additions to the family, look for a mouse or rat with a soft, silky coat; bright eyes that are free of discharge; and healthy-looking feet, ears, nose and visible areas of skin. The fine pet prospect should present a picture of all-around good health and an alert and lively demeanor, especially apparent in a rat that runs to the cage bars begging you to take it home. If a rat is what you are seeking, your mission is not only to choose a healthy pet, but also one that is curious about humans in general and interested in you specifically.

Listen to the animal's breathing, as well. Rats and mice are especially prone to respiratory problems, usually caused by contact with infected animals or a habitat's poor hygiene. Listen for wheezy, rattly breathing and watch for excessive sneezing. You must practice the same vigilance when caring for these animals at home, for some of the bacterial infections that can affect a rat's or mouse's respiratory tract can be treated, or at least controlled, with antibiotics.

Mice and rats are social animals that, by nature, live in colonies. Keeping two or more together will enable the little animals to interact, play and groom as dictated by their social instincts. A rat, for example, in a home where its owners are frequently away, will fare best if housed with a companion.

Rat fanciers are quick to emphasize that the rat-to-rat relationship in a multi-rat domicile will in no way diminish the rat's bond to its owner, as long as that owner continues to make the effort to spend time with his or her pets on a regular basis. Again, be sure the animals you house together are of the same sex or you may experience a rodent population explosion in a matter of weeks.

LIVING WITH YOUR RODENT

As they have made very obvious throughout history, rats and mice are extremely well adapted to living with humans. Today they happily do so in the role of family pet, filling a void in the lives of individuals who want a pet that is warm, fuzzy and interactive, but who, given any number of restrictions, cannot have a typical cat or dog. For these people, a cute, perhaps even cuddly, mouse or rat can be a perfect—and petite—answer to fill that longing. Such individuals often end up so enamored of these animals that they choose to live with them for years to come, even when they find themselves in a situation amenable to the keeping of more traditional pet species.

Admittedly, the temperaments of rats and mice differ between species, as should your expectations of their individual world views. But proper care is identical for both. When bringing a new rat or mouse home, for example, allow it a few days to get adjusted to its new home and its new owner. Avoid loud noises or abrupt movements, and after a few days you may begin to increase the level and the nature of interaction.

Rats and mice usually bite only out of fear, not anger, so preventing fear is an honorable goal in caring for these small animals. Remain quiet and calm. Be the ideal companion, and show it through your gentle actions that you are one to be trusted.

Depending on each particular animal's personality, after a few days, you may try putting your hand into the cage and keeping it very still. This is not a good idea for shy animals that might be frightened by the act, but a more gregarious, curious critter, more likely a rat than a mouse, will come forward to explore your hand, perhaps nibble it a bit, and get acquainted with your scent. Foster such an inquisitive attitude by allowing it to take treats from

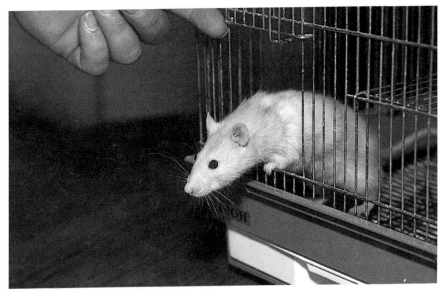

A well-socialized pet will willingly come to the door of its cage for the opportunity to explore the great outdoors. *Michael A. Siino*

your hand (a practice generally more successful with rats than with mice), so it learns to associate sweet rewards with your presence.

Speak softly and, whenever you handle or approach the animal, call it by name and reinforce the positive aspect of the moment with a favorite treat (many use a Cheerio™, but don't overdo it). Rats can also be trained to come to you with such rewards. The secret is patience and short training sessions, equally effective when teaching the rat to sit on your lap and ride on your shoulder.

Daily interactions can help keep rats and mice very tame. A healthy, well-socialized mouse may learn to enjoy gentle handling, but if it prefers to remain a homebody, respect that inclination and handle the animal only when necessary. Whenever you hold a pet mouse or rat, do so very gently, supporting its body in your hands. Make sure children are supervised when handling these animals, which may be injured by a sudden drop or an inadvertent squeeze.

So should you respect these animals' space. When you want or need to hold them, some prefer that you not invade their habitat, their territory, with your hand. While a friendly rat will probably jump out to you the moment you open the door, a more timid animal, typically a mouse, may prefer being coaxed out onto your hand rather than being lifted from a place it associates with security and privacy. A treat may further convince this shy one. Such practices will help the animal build trust in its handler and maintain a secure association with its cage.

Your Rodent in Your Home

Each mouse and rat harbors individual opinions on handling and play. While it is dangerous to allow mice to run free in the house because of their tiny size and their inclination to hide in spots where they can never be found, most rats enjoy the liberty and are typically more interested in participating in your activities than in seeking unusual hiding places. You must remember, however, that these animals are rodents and will gnaw anything should the urge come upon them, whether that anything is the leg of a valuable antique chair or a live electrical cord.

Allowing rats to run free and unsupervised throughout the house is to court disaster. The rat may not only feel compelled to chew, but it may also become inadvertently trapped in an unknown nook or cranny it discovers while exploring, or be stepped on by a visitor who is not subconsciously attuned to watching for rats underfoot. Supervision is mandatory.

Some rats have even been known to befriend the family cat or dog, but if your rat shows this propensity, all interactions must be carefully supervised. It's also important before even considering introducing the rat to these animals, which are, after all, predators, to evaluate the other pets' personalities. Some dogs are quite predatory toward rodents, and we need not even discuss the age-old relationship between rodents and cats. As for mice, it's best never even to entertain the idea of such introductions. There is no point to subjecting the mouse to an experience that will only lead to trauma and distrust.

That trauma comes from the fact that in nature rats and mice are hunted and threatened by a great many predators, including the human predator, yet they are armed with few defenses. The staggering breeding rates of rats and mice is actually an evolutionary means of survival for these species, their ability to procreate quickly and abundantly serving as an effective mechanism to protect the vigor of their populations. They breed rapidly to keep their populations healthy. This has worked beautifully for their numbers, but it can cause trouble when one takes a pair as pets.

Rats and mice do enjoy each others' company, but great care must be taken when introducing an animal to an existing community (males may have trouble cohabiting unless they were raised together as youngsters). Isolate the newcomer for at least three weeks to ensure that it is not ill or carrying parasites that might affect the established population.

The same precautions are in order should you notice possible signs of respiratory problems in one of the animals. The suspect should be removed immediately and isolated in a hospital cage, while the main cage is cleaned and disinfected to help prevent contagion.

HEALTHY HOUSING

Rats and mice spend a great deal of time at home in the habitat you provide for them. While a rat can enjoy time outside with its human family, mice, being more timid and consummate escape artists/hiders, will be spending far more time in their habitat than their rat brethren.

The ideal mouse house or rat retreat is a spacious, well-ventilated gnaw-proof cage, or a fish tank with a well-ventilated, tight-fitting screen top. Avoid wood cages that can and will be chewed to smithereens in no time, and beware of wire-bottomed cages with one-inch-by-half-inch mesh in which a mouse or rat can catch and break a leg. A safer wire-bottomed cage is one with a bottom of half-inch square mesh. Safer yet is a solid-bottomed bird cage or more traditionally styled wire cages with solid bottoms that can slide out for cleaning and bedding changes.

While glass fish tanks offer a nice setting for viewing, even some owners with a longtime allegiance to this setup are now switching to wire cages because of the ample ventilation they provide. Ventilation, many believe, helps prevent respiratory problems.

Rats may also enjoy a vertical, multilevel setup that allows them to jump from level to level, an ideal activity for this animal that so enjoys athletic activity. But just as you must be careful with the mesh flooring of wire cages, so must you ensure that the shelves be of either solid material or tightly woven mesh wire to ensure the rat will not catch a leg and be injured.

If a fish tank is your habitat of choice, it must have a top that cannot be pushed off by a wily rat or an inquisitive cat. A screen framed in wood, held down by a brick or clips on the side, makes a good top, as do custom-made tops that can be fitted to the individual habitat.

The cage or tank should be placed in a spot out of drafts and away from direct sunlight or high humidity, all of which can lead to respiratory trouble. A table, a dresser or a shelf will provide a good foundation, as long as they prove inaccessible to the prying paws of would-be canine and feline predators that also happen to share the home. Keep the cage in an area where the external temperature ranges from about 70 to 78 degrees Fahrenheit, about the same temperatures where we humans are most comfortable.

Mice, and some rats, enjoy burrowing, so provide these pets with a habitat where they can do so. The secret is in the bedding. Avoid cedar or pine shavings as bedding, as these can cause respiratory problems or damage organs. Aspen shavings and other aspen products are preferable, as are special sanitary products like shredded paper or alfalfa pellets. Fill the cage or tank bottom with about two or three inches of the bedding, which will keep the animal cozy and content by allowing it to burrow safely. As a special treat, you can supplement the bedding with some clean, dry hay as nesting material and your pets will be in seventh heaven.

Mice and rats like to burrow, so give them plenty of bedding in which to do it, preferably aspen shavings, alfalfa pellets or shredded sanitary paper. *Michael A. Siino*

The habitat must be large enough to provide the animal with separate areas for sleeping, eating and exercise. Most of these animals will also defecate and urinate in the same spot each time, usually a corner far from the eating and sleeping areas. You may place a litter box there, or, if the flooring is solid and covered with bedding material, place a thicker layer of bedding in that chosen spot so you can remove soiled material each day and thus help control odor.

If keeping more than one mouse or rat, the habitat must be large enough for all to coexist contentedly. Overpopulation leads to stress, panic and even causes illness. Provide the animals with at least one square foot of cage floor space for each mouse, and two square feet for each rat. The larger the habitat the better, both for the well-being and contentment of the mice and rats, and for the visual enjoyment of the owner.

Home Decorating

Every rat, and especially every mouse, from time to time craves some privacy. To satisfy this need, furnish the animals' habitat with a sleeping box, either a commercially produced covered bed from a pet supply store or, as a less expensive option, one made from an everyday household container made of nontoxic material such as a jar or a cylindrical oatmeal container. Regardless of what you choose, a rat or a mouse does need a bed, especially if it is in a cage with a wire bottom that cannot be covered with bedding. Constant contact with that flooring can cause sores on the animal's feet.

Watch a couple of mice or rats for a few minutes, and you realize very quickly that these animals can get bored just as can a dog or a cat. Aside from fulfilling their profound sense of fun, extracurricular activities also provide preventive therapeutic services for both their physical and psychological well-being.

Accessorizing is easy enough. Simply provide the animals with toys that fit their taste and objects for gnawing. Avoid soft plastic items that will inevitably be chewed and shredded, and perhaps cause a potentially fatal intestinal blockage. Gnawing is as natural to these animals as breathing; it cannot be trained out of them, nor should it be punished. Instead, satisfy those rodent gnawing urges positively with safe items, such as blocks of unpainted hardwood, hard rubber bones made for dogs or pesticide-free branches from fruit trees.

To vent excess energy, most rats and mice also enjoy an occasional spin on an exercise wheel. The rats' exercise wheel must also obviously be larger than that for a mouse, ideally about a foot or so in diameter. Though we superior humans may tease about the rodent intellect and its fascination for these wheels that travel nowhere, how different is it from our own habit of spending hours on a stationary bicycle or a treadmill? So emerges another similarity between us and our rodent friends.

Rats especially tend to enjoy athletic activities: ladders to climb, shelves to traverse. Just beware of gaps or holes in and around such items, in which a small leg or foot can be trapped or broken.

A fun-loving, mischievous mouse or rat may also enjoy the addition of cardboard boxes, cardboard tubes (those from a paper towel roll for rats, from toilet paper for mice) and large PVC pipe segments for tunneling and hiding. Kelle Steward of the American Fancy Rat and Mouse Association once lived with a rat whose favorite toy was an old sock. Kelle would place the sock in the cage, the rat would wiggle its way in, turn itself around at the toe and then wiggle its way to the opening where it would remain happily with its head peeking out of its favorite sock.

And of course never underestimate the therapeutic value of a companion mouse or rat, its presence permitting the communal games and mutual grooming so natural to these rodents' nature.

FEEDING YOUR RATS OR MICE

Rats and mice have phenomenally high metabolic rates and must have food available to them at all times. Every few hours they must eat. The good news is that providing them with the proper sustenance is a breeze.

Although we come to believe from our experiences with "pest" rodents that mice and rats will eat virtually anything, this does not mean you should follow this philosophy in feeding pet mice and rats. Forego sweets, junk food or leftovers, and opt instead for a basic diet of high-quality, commercially available pelleted foods designed for laboratory rodents. Another option embraced by many breeders are Lablocks™, which will not only provide proper nutrition, but also, because of their hard texture, help hone the teeth. Some owners supplement this foundation diet several times a week with a ration of a high-quality grain mixture available at pet supply stores.

You can further supplement the diet, and win your pet's eternal devotion, with dry whole wheat bread and fresh, clean fruits and vegetables: broccoli, the green sections of bok choy, a cooked sweet potato, a grape or a slice of banana. Seeds and nuts can become beloved treats, but, as rich as they are, they should be fed sparingly. A better treat alternative is cooked spaghetti. Rats particularly love the stuff, especially when it wiggles, which, according to Debbie Ducommun of the Rat Fan Club, seems to incite some type of predatory response in the animals.

As you can see, a varied diet will entertain these animals and keep them content. Just make sure to remove all uneaten fresh foods the day after placing them in the cage to prevent contamination.

Regardless of what you are feeding your rodent pets, the foods must be fresh. Resist the temptation to buy commercial feed in bulk if you are caring for only a few mice or rats and don't expect to use it up quickly. The food will become musty and stale with age.

Feed rats and mice from food dishes or from racks that hang from the cage wall. Throwing food in from the top of the cage fosters bad habits of begging and biting. Feed mice and rats in a dish that is easy to clean and heavy enough that it cannot be tipped over by a boisterous animal; avoid soft plastic dishes that can be shredded by a rodent in the mood to chew.

You must of course also supply this pet with an ample supply of fresh clean water at all times, best offered in a traditional water bottle with a metal spout. Change the water daily, and, while you're at it, check the spout to make sure it isn't clogged. If water is offered in a dish, the requirements are identical to those for feeding dishes: heavy and chew-resistant.

Though rats and mice need to eat frequently, feeding times can be morning and evening; it is not necessary to change their food every few hours. Water, however, should be available at all times.

Rats and mice can be left alone for the weekend and perhaps as long as three or four days if need be, but it is critical that the owner ensure that the water bottle be in proper operational order and that enough food is left behind. A water bottle is preferable because water in a dish will become soiled or spill quickly. Even a bottle left longer than a few days could clog or leak, which is in fact the most dangerous thing that could happen in an owner's absence.

Mouse and rat shows are popular events, featuring what are referred to as "fancy" mice and rats, such as the satin mouse on the left and the hairless rats on the right. *Michael A. Siino*

KEEPING YOUR PET RODENTS CLEAN

Although traditionally associated with such words as filth and vermin, rats and mice actually thrive on cleanliness. There is a direct correlation between an unclean habitat and an ill rat or mouse. Practicing consistent sanitation habits is the key to keeping a rodent of this type happy and to preserving its good health.

Although urine, especially a male's urine, can smell quite strong, especially in the case of a rat with a propensity to scent mark its territory, most of these pets generally do not present an extreme odor problem. If you do notice an unpleasant smell, the cage is probably to blame, for odor will emanate from a cage that is not being cleaned properly or frequently enough. That situation is easily remedied.

Frequency of cleaning is dictated by the individual animals' habits. For example, the bedding in a scent marker's habitat will have to be changed more frequently than that of an animal that doesn't share that particular habit. The bedding for an animal that frequently hides its food throughout the cage will also have to be changed more frequently.

In general, every two or three days is a good schedule to follow in changing the bedding, but it may be required more often for mice, which tend to be more susceptible to illness than rats. Some owners further control odor and preserve bedding freshness by spreading a light layer of cat litter or baking soda beneath the bedding to help absorb odors and moisture.

The entire cleaning regimen is best conducted according to a schedule. Most rats and mice will thrive if their food dishes and water bottle are cleaned daily, the bedding changed every few days and the cage structure and accessories cleaned and disinfected every week (twice a week if you can).

When it's time for a thorough cleaning of the cage or tank, remove and relocate the resident animals to a temporary small holding cage. After disposing of the bedding and nesting material, clean the glass of a fish tank with a traditional cleaning solution or a bleach-and-water mixture; just remember to rinse all residues away and dry the tank completely before rebedding and returning the animals to their home. Dispose of the bedding from a wire cage, scrub it with either hot soap and water or a bleach-and-water mixture, rinse it well, dry it well, and then place a new layer of fresh, clean bedding on the cage floor. Now the animals may come home.

In addition to the cleaning of the food dishes and water bottle, daily duties include removing soiled bedding; dirty, worn gnawing material; and leftover or uneaten food. This should be supplemented with the more thorough disinfection on a weekly basis.

As for the animals' personal hygiene, they will usually take care of that themselves, cleaning themselves constantly like small cats. If you would like to help out, you can brush the animal gently with a soft-bristle toothbrush—assuming, of course, that the animal is willing. Never force the issue.

Bathing is not generally recommended for these animals, but some owners will occasionally bathe a rat, especially if it is scheduled to be shown. When bathing a rat, use only a very mild, gentle shampoo, which must be rinsed thoroughly from the small animal. Following the bath, allow the rat to dry thoroughly in a warm place, and do not permit it to catch a chill. As for mice, they should be left to their own devices; they are too small to bathe, too stress-prone to be bathed and too susceptible to the respiratory illness bathing can cause.

Another concern that may worm its way into your relationship with a rat or a mouse is the discovery of external parasites, such as mites and fleas on or around the animal. Such infestations can represent an annoyance as well as a health threat.

At the first sign of external parasites, treat the animals with a control product formulated specifically for safe use on small rodents. Use the product sparingly and only as directed. At the same time, remove the animal(s) from the primary cage, and, while the rats or mice are away, discard the old bedding and clean and disinfect both the cage and its furnishings. You must take great care when using chemicals or pesticides around rodents. They are extremely sensitive to such substances and can perish from overexposure to them.

Salamanders are ancient amphibians that have evolved in a variety of colors and patterns. This is a northern red salamander, whose skin is a neon shade of red.
David G. Barker

CHAPTER 10

Up From the Ooze: The Salamander

Hundreds of millions of years ago, the only creatures to inhabit the earth were those beneath the vast oceans that covered the planet. Then, one day, out from the primordial pool, appeared a small head.

Looking back on that day, we hypothesize now that this was a small, obviously fish-like creature, an anomaly born of its kind with leg-like structures that would allow it to traverse the land, and a breathing apparatus that could respirate oxygen taken in from the open atmosphere. On that momentous day almost 400 million years ago, life on land was born.

Scientists today believe that that first pioneer must have been very much like the animals we now refer to as amphibians. Only an animal such as this would have been able to bridge the gap between breathing in water and breathing in the open air. This patriarch (or matriarch, as the case may have been), would unknowingly spawn all terrestrial life on our planet. That single act of emerging from the water to the land would beget, over millions of years, distinct families of amphibians, reptiles, insects, spiders, birds and, finally, mammals, including the human mammal.

What makes this story even more fascinating is that living among us today are what are believed to be the most distinctly direct descendants of those first land dwellers, animals that hundreds of millions of years later, continue to exhibit the characteristics that led those first amphibians to their—and our—destiny on land. That animal is the salamander.

So what does this tell us? That our species may thank the salamander for our very existence? Perhaps. We will never know for sure. All we might guess (and, of course, all will never agree) is that the first land animals on our planet were probably amphibians, and that those amphibians probably looked

The Salamander as a Pet

	Light	1	2	3	4	5	Heavy
TIME COMMITMENT			🐴				
MAINTENANCE Grooming		🐴					
Feeding					🐴		
General Clean-Up				🐴			
SUITABILITY TO CHILDREN Ages Infant-5		🐴					
Ages 5-10			🐴				
Over 10					🐴		
SOCIABILITY			🐴				
EXPENSE OF KEEPING			🐴				

quite similar to the salamanders that we are today likely to spot in damp, secluded, forested woodlands throughout the world. Consequently, while the lizard families may transport us back in time to the age of the dinosaurs, the amphibians carry us back even further, perhaps even to our very own beginnings.

If nothing more, this should at least increase the respect we offer an animal that is often maligned, dismissed as slimy, disgusting and ugly. Fortunately, there are those who can see beyond such unfounded notions to the natural beauty and evolutionary significance of the salamander. It is these individuals who embrace these ancient souls and take the animals into their homes as reminders of what once was—and what almost wasn't.

THE AMPHIBIAN FAMILY

A fascinating family are the amphibians. Obviously one of the oldest families, as well, the amphibians are presumed to have evolved very early on into a niche very much like the one they continue to occupy today. While much is yet to be learned about them, and while statements about them must invariably be tempered with caution because facts that apply to most species cannot be applied to all, these are profoundly ancient animals about which some generalities may be made.

Considered somewhere between fish and reptiles physiologically, most amphibian species in one way or another employ water for their breeding practices. Their young spend their formative time in water, ultimately undergoing a metamorphosis that will prepare them for life on land as mature beings.

Some amphibians, though adapted to the air of the land, will spend a great deal of time in the water as adults, while others will carry on primarily as terrestrial creatures. But whether frogs, toads, salamanders, newts or the other more exotic amphibian strains, all will be driven throughout their lives by an ancient calling. A voice that reminds them every day to protect their sensitive skins from dehydration—and, hence, death. These animals are far more likely, then, to be found in quiet, dark, damp secluded areas than they are basking on a beach.

In captivity, the more aquatic species of amphibians, such as aquatic frogs and newts, require a habitat with water pools that must be maintained very much as a fish tank would be (complete with filtration systems), offering them room to swim, yet access to land. Our focus, however, is the more terrestrial amphibians, namely, the salamanders.

The western tiger salamander is a popular pet species. Its skin is cream colored with bold black stripes, reminiscent of a tiger. *David G. Barker*

Though salamanders are considered quite close in appearance and character to their aquatic cousins the newts, the term salamander typically refers to the more terrestrial of the two—the animals that spend most of their time on land (and that are thus the easier of the two to care for). These are decidedly unusual-looking animals, not nearly as whimsical in appearance as the more popular frogs and toads, but animals that command attention and respect of their own.

ABOUT SALAMANDERS

Since that first courageous soul that made a foray onto land those many eons ago, hundreds of salamander species now populate the globe, many of them residing quietly and secretly in the forests, woodlands and meadows of North America. Salamanders worldwide run the gamut in size, from species that can grow several feet in length, to the more manageable pet species, such as the popular fire and tiger salamanders that average about seven to fifteen inches. Salamanders vary greatly in color and natural habitat, as well, yet all are relatively docile creatures.

Though some salamanders have toxins in their skin to repel predators (virtually their only defense mechanism aside from a natural inclination to hide), salamanders present no threat to humans. The same cannot, however, be said for the effect of humans on salamanders, given our species' propensity to handle animals that really shouldn't be handled, our habit of keeping amphibians in captive conditions that could not be worse for them and, as a population, our compulsion to destroy natural salamander habitats and thus dramatically reduce their wild populations.

Although it is often mistaken for a lizard by those who do not understand the distinct differences between amphibians and reptiles, the classic salamander sports a plump, longish, cylindrically shaped physique with a relatively large head; a longish muscular tail; and legs sprouted from its side, almost perpendicular from its body. With feet that remind one of human hands, salamanders usually crawl on land slowly in a unique almost snakelike zigzag pattern, twisting their bodies from side to side, those handlike appendages providing both balance and propulsion.

While all members of the same family, salamanders are unique from one another in their early development. Some are hatched underwater with gills that allow them to breathe within that environment, others may hatch instead in a moist and hidden terrestrial site and some even develop within their mother's body. Salamanders do undergo a metamorphosis, not one as dramatic as happens with the frog or the toad, but a change that, in most cases, will prepare them for life as land animals with the breathing apparatuses to match. Those aquatically hatched salamanders, for example, will lose the gills of their larval stage and go on to adulthood breathing air on land.

The care of salamanders requires the owner to gather as much information as possible about the particular species that has come to reside in his or her home. What type of environment does it come from? What does it eat in the wild? Only this way can the animal be treated to a natural living situation that resembles as closely as possible the one it would experience in the wild. Diet, housing and atmosphere all play critical roles, all planned and executed with an overriding concern for the health of the salamander's skin.

THE SALAMANDER'S OUTSIDES

Though often described as "slimy," a salamander's skin, depending on species, may be vibrantly patterned and colored or conservatively camouflaged. It may be rough or smooth, and while some feel fairly dry to the touch, others might indeed be referred to as slimy. The sliminess of the salamander's skin is a matter of life and death for the salamander.

The salamander's "slimy" skin protects it from its environment and natural predators. In captivity, it's important to furnish salamanders with some moist leaves and moss in which they can hide and stay wet. *David G. Barker*

Perhaps we humans would respect the sanctity of the salamander's skin a bit more if we would realize the miraculous role it plays in the protection of the salamander. For one, this animal breathes through its skin, and it must be moist to facilitate this. Simply put, the salamander takes in oxygen at the surface of its skin and in the lining of its mouth. While for some species, lungs play a role in breathing as well, some salamander species never develop lungs.

Aside from its vital role in respiration, the salamander's skin is also extremely sensitive to subtle sensations it picks up from its environment, alerting the animal to potentially dangerous situations or perhaps to the arrival of that night's dinner. In addition, the skin absorbs moisture from the environment to keep the animal properly hydrated. Mucus-producing glands within the skin help keep the surface of the skin moist and preserve that hydration, thus producing a shiny look to the skin, or, in some species, a moist layer of protective slime.

A lack of moisture—in some species, a lack of slime—will impair the life-giving functions of the skin, and thus, the health and functioning of the body at large. Any way you look at it the skin is both tool and protective device, keeping the salamander oxygenated, hydrated, nourished and safe from would-be predators. A vital organ in every sense of the word.

To protect that vital organ, salamanders in the wild naturally seek out cooler temperatures and sheltered living situations. Only that way may they protect their skin, and thus their entire system, from fatal or certainly debilitating dehydration. What this tells the keeper of a salamander is that to protect this animal's skin and to prevent stress that can lead to illness, the salamander should have ample opportunity to hide within its terrarium, and temperatures within that habitat should be maintained at about 75 degrees Fahrenheit (or preferably lower). In other words, this animal should fare well within the normal room temperatures of most typical human households.

HANDLING A SALAMANDER

If you truly respect the salamander's skin, you will naturally understand why this animal should not be subjected to handling any more than is necessary. These are animals better suited to life within a well-appointed terrarium where they may live contentedly while their owners look on. Gratuitous handling can lead to salamander stress and even damage that sensitive skin, the vital organ that the salamander spends its life protecting.

For obvious reasons, salamanders do not appreciate the warmth of a human hand, plus the sweat upon that hand can be irritating to the salamander's skin. If you must handle the animal, there are certain protocols you must follow.

First, wash your hands thoroughly. Rinse them well and dry them well to ensure no soap residue remains embedded in your skin, as that might irritate the salamander's skin. Then, do your pet a favor and moisten your hands with water prior to actual contact (some handlers don moistened latex gloves to protect the animal even further). This will help protect the skin and perhaps make the experience more pleasant for the salamander.

While handling should be done only as necessary, there are times you must remove the animal from its habitat, say at salamander house cleaning time or for a veterinary checkup. All handling must be done gently and quietly.

Because direct hand-to-salamander contact can be stressful for the animal, you might want to forego the direct contact altogether in favor of a method by which you usher the salamander gently into a clean plastic box outfitted with some moist sphagnum moss for hiding and holes in the top for ventilation. Close the box securely, and you have in one swift move reduced and even prevented unnecessary stress, alleviated the risk of dropping the animal and protected its skin, all at the same time.

WATCHING FOR FUNGAL INFECTION

Another time when you will have to remove the salamander from its happy home is if you notice signs of health problems. The most common of these is a fungal infection. These can occur when the salamander is injured in a squabble with a fellow amphibian, is cut by an object within its habitat, or, as is most commonly the case, by unhygienic habitat conditions.

If you spot a patch of white fuzz on your salamander's skin, your pet has probably contracted a fungal infection. Remove the salamander from its habitat immediately and place it in a properly appointed holding tank (quick removal is especially critical if other salamanders share its abode because fungal infections are highly contagious). As you take care of the homefront, cleaning and disinfecting the enclosure, a veterinarian skilled in the treatment of amphibians can prescribe an appropriate treatment for the patient itself. Just remember that the earlier you seek treatment, preferably at the first sign of something amiss, whether it be internal or external, the better the animal's chances of recovery.

To reduce your own role as a potential carrier of contagion within a multi-amphibian household—and to prevent irritating one salamander species with the skin toxins of another—wash your hands thoroughly between handling of each animal or their habitat and house each species separately to protect their respective skins.

As for your own skin, whenever you touch a salamander or any item within its habitat, make sure you wash your hands both before and after you do so. Though not venomous, irritating toxins in the animal's skin can irritate human eyes or open cuts.

The safest rule of thumb for all concerned is to handle salamanders only as necessary, wash your hands thoroughly before holding the salamander to protect its skin and wash them again after handling to protect yours.

SELECTING A SALAMANDER

Salamanders are typically named as one of the pet species easiest to care for, often, unfortunately, by people who don't understand the private natures of these creatures or just exactly what they do require. Despite this, they are not unusually demanding pets, and they may actually be less expensive to purchase than many reptile species or even than their fellow amphibians in the frog and toad family.

Despite their quiet natures, salamanders are extremely prone to stress and thus to the illnesses stress can induce. Stress is typically caused by unhygienic, unnatural surroundings (i.e., too much light, too warm of air temperatures or an absence of hiding places). Obtaining a salamander from a reputable source, then, is obviously of critical importance in the early stages of your relationship with an animal of this kind.

Pet stores, especially those that specialize in reptiles and amphibians, are the most obvious source for salamanders, especially for fine specimens now being bred in captivity. But given the fact that salamanders are native to many regions of the United States, some people collect them from their native habitats. There is, however, some controversy involved in this practice.

When collected from their homes, salamanders will naturally be more prone to stress than will one who was hatched and raised in an environment managed by humans. Wild salamanders are also more likely to be carriers of disease or parasites. But beyond this is the issue of long-term commitment, for too often, people who collect salamanders this way, upon discovering that the animal's care requirements are more complex than they expected or upon realizing that the novelty of the animal has worn off, release them back into the wild.

Unfortunately, some owners have been known to do this with non-native salamander species, as well. This is, of course, cruel in that it subjects the animal to an environment for which millions of years of evolution have not prepared it, plus it can disrupt the lives of the other native species the salamander meets there. Native animals released after exposure to a human domicile may carry with them parasites or disease that can then affect the rest of the wild population.

Yes, it takes some effort to consider carefully one's decision to obtain a pet, even a pet you might collect from your own backyard, but think of the animal. Though sometimes unfairly labeled as lowly and base by those who do not appreciate its significance in the grand zoological and ecological scheme of life on this planet, the salamander deserves such considerations.

Only if you are willing to commit to its care should you take it into your home in the first place. To view it as a temporary pet or as one that is somehow less valuable or does not need veterinary care, is unfair to the salamander. This can not only fatally stress the animal, but can lead to the destruction of others from its home should you choose to release it back where it came from. If, on the other hand, you find yourself truly enchanted by this fascinating creature, the salamander can make a wonderful pet.

What a Healthy Salamander Looks Like

Whether seeking a salamander in the wild or through a commercial source, evidence that an animal you are evaluating has been kept in a clean environment with the proper temperatures, humidity levels and nutrition may be seen in bright, clear eyes; a plump physique; and skin that is smooth, clear and free of lesions or patches of fuzzy white growths. If you do notice those telltale white splotches that typically indicate fungal infection, avoid the affected animal as well as any others from its display tank.

When selecting items for your salamander's terrarium, make sure none of them has sharp edges, which can cut or scrape this animal's delicate skin. *David G. Barker*

Travel can be stressful for even a healthy animal, so bring your new pet home in an appropriately outfitted receptacle: a clean plastic box or glass jar with a securely fitting, well-ventilated top and a clump of moistened sphagnum moss inside for hiding—a security blanket, if you will. Be very careful to keep this receptacle out of direct sunlight or any heat source that will overheat the animal; in other words, don't buy a salamander and run off to the beach, leaving your new pet in the car while you play. Rather, get the animal home and installed in its new habitat, which you should have prepared ahead of time with the appropriate flooring and hiding places. Follow this game plan and you will dramatically reduce the natural stress a salamander will experience from such a disruption to its routine.

SETTING UP THE TERRARIUM

Because this is not a pet that either needs or thrives on constant handling, setting up a lovely environment in which it may be observed is the kindest and most constructive avenue to take toward its responsible care.

For the primarily terrestrial salamander, your goal is to re-create what the animal would seek out and experience in the wild, the next best thing to home. For most this means providing the animal with an almost bog-like environment with a soft, moist, mossy floor and live leafy plants for hiding. These plants should ideally be planted in separate pots embedded in the flooring of the terrarium rather than planted directly into the flooring itself, so you can remove them and change them as needed.

Piles of leaves, driftwood, stone caves, smooth rocks and moss piles will also be greatly appreciated by a salamander who is driven by that ancient desire to protect its skin and to spend its days hiding, burrowing and otherwise avoiding the sun and the bright lights of civilization. Forget that salamanders gravitate toward areas that are quiet, damp and secluded and neglect to provide them with these comforts, and you are asking for both trouble and a salamander with a very short lifespan.

You may further assist your salamander in its skin-protecting mission by ensuring that any item you place in the terrarium is free of sharp edges that might cut the animal's skin, that such items are securely anchored within the flooring and that they are disinfected before making their debut within the habitat.

Needless to say, a terrarium of this kind can be an attractive addition to your household decor, while at the same time providing your amphibious pet with its optimum domicile. That habitat will only be ideal, however, if it includes a water source, which will also help to humidify the air of the terrarium. This will be far less water than you would offer an aquatic frog or a newt, but the salamander should have a shallow dish of water well anchored in the substrate of the habitat. The bottom dish section of a flower pot should fill this bill quite nicely. Change the water daily, and you're in business.

As for the structure of the habitat, a glass fish tank with a well-ventilated top (perhaps a securely fitting, wood-lined, small-mesh screen top) will help maintain that critical balance between ventilation and humidity required to keep the salamander healthy.

The tank should be carpeted with a soft, woodland flooring, preferably of sphagnum moss or soft shredded bark (no cedar, which may be too aromatic, or wood chips, which are too sharp). Moss can also be used in a layered flooring system implemented by many herpetologists. In this system several inches of moss are placed on top of a layer of sanitized gravel (for drainage); both of these layers are then placed above a grate (to further facilitate drainage). While gravel can be a good drainage element or an appropriate flooring for aquatic species of amphibians, it can be dangerous as the primary flooring material for terrestrial species because the animals might accidentally ingest it.

All in all, sphagnum moss is an excellent all-around flooring material because it holds moisture, it's easy on the salamander's feet and it's easy on an owner's bank account because it is inexpensive enough to be changed regularly, thus facilitating the cleanliness of the environment. It also provides an excellent medium for burrowing.

And while we're on the subject of moss, most salamanders universally agree that there is nothing better than a hill of moss within their enclosures for a hiding place/shelter. This can be a handy tool for you, as well, in that you may mist this moss every other day or so to help keep the entire enclosure properly hydrated.

Humid, but not too Moist

Some owners take the quest for humidity too far by misting the entire enclosure on a daily basis. This results in an enclosure that is too moist and undeniably sloppy, which subsequently opens the door for infestations of bacteria and fungi—and an epidemic of sick salamanders. Misting only the hill of moss every other day, plus the presence of the water dish, will keep the moisture under control while still providing the resident salamander with what it needs in terms of hydration.

While the air should be somewhat moist within the terrarium, so must it be cool, generally the same temperatures we maintain for ourselves in our homes, about 68 to 75 degrees Fahrenheit. While for obvious reasons you must never place a salamander or its enclosure in direct sunlight (dehydration and overheating, remember?), salamanders do seem to appreciate a natural photoperiod, meaning a natural number of daylight hours versus a natural

Salamanders are carnivores, and crickets are an essential part of their diet. *Michael A. Siino*

number of hours of darkness. A fluorescent light positioned above the enclosure during the daytime will provide the resident animal with full-spectrum light that will simulate sunlight without producing dehydrating heat.

As we have seen, you must also keep the tank clean. This means that to keep fungi and bacteria at bay within the animal's moist environment, you should remove soiled flooring daily, remove uneaten food items every day, and when you do a wholesale cleaning and disinfecting of the tank, rinse every structure and item *completely*, for chemical residues can be incredibly irritating and even damaging to a salamander's skin.

FEEDING A SALAMANDER

It may take a while for your pet salamander to settle down and adjust to its new surroundings, especially if it is newly collected from the wild, unaccustomed to captive life.

If the salamander seems to require some wind-down time (and most do), allow your new pet to remain quiet and unmolested within its enclosure for a few days. Once it does come around and its appetite kicks in, you will discover why these animals have such reputations as easy feeders, their menu including some of the most plentiful items on earth. These are not, mind you, items you are likely to find in your own refrigerator; however, you might find them in your backyard or at a local bait shop.

Although salamanders are not typically responsive to their human handlers, they have been known to be so, or at least to exhibit a bit of excitement, when it's time to eat. Like all amphibians, salamanders are classic carnivores. Their diets consist of live prey, a grim thought to many pet owners, but one that must be accepted if you are to care for these animals properly.

Although some have been known to take pieces of meat when offered, only the whole body of insects, worms and such will supply salamanders with the balance of nutrients that they require. Their diets and their nutritional needs have been millions of years in the making. You cannot hope to change this within your household in a few months or even years, simply because their tastes make you squeamish.

Salamanders usually move with a slow grace, a characteristic that tends to paint their eating habits as well. They typically approach their food slowly, then make a sudden grab, trapping food items within their wide mouths. The targets of this activity are varied. Salamanders enjoy dining on crickets, earthworms (particularly night crawlers), virtually any type of insect, mealworms, fruit flies, termites and some may even be inclined to ingest fellow amphibians.

Most of these foodstuffs are available commercially from pet supply stores and, in the case of worms, bait and aquarium shops. Some amphibian devotees who get more and more enmeshed in this hobby learn to cultivate their own strains of their pets' foods. Many harvest their own, as well, supplementing the crickets and worms they purchase for their pets with flying insects, worms and even termites they collect themselves from the great outdoors.

Feed your salamander once a day, but be conservative. You want to be careful not to overfeed by offering it more than it can take in one sitting. And remember, any item it chooses not to take, or any that end up drowned in the water dish, should be removed daily to prevent unsanitary conditions within the habitat.

Another good rule of thumb is to offer your pet a vitamin/mineral supplement once or twice a week. Of course, you can't do this by offering it a chewable orange tablet in the shape of a popular cartoon character, but the method you can use is just as simple. Sprinkle the food, particularly moist night crawlers and crickets, with a fine vitamin/mineral supplement powder formulated especially for reptiles and amphibians. Ensuring that the commercially purchased crickets you feed are themselves well-fed and well-hydrated may also help ensure that your pet receives a healthy diet, for, after all, salamanders are what they eat.

If beauty is in the eye of the beholder, then tarantula enthusiasts can't help but find this Mexican redknee with its plump abdomen and eight well-bristled legs a vision of loveliness. *Michael A. Siino*

CHAPTER 11

Eight-Legged Legend: The Tarantula

When most people consider the word "pet," the image of a soft, fuzzy animal comes to mind. But does that image still apply when the soft fuzzy pet has eight legs and feeds mostly on live prey?

This eight-legged pet with a taste for meat is, if you haven't guessed, the tarantula, legendary star of television, film and folklore. Only the most sheltered among us are unacquainted with the tarantula, that giant fuzzy spider that inspires images of old haunted houses, deserted graveyards and the delicious experience of watching scary old movies on a dark and stormy night. But what most of us think we know about the spider itself is simply the product of our own and others' imaginations. Very little of it is grounded in fact.

Yes, horror stories do abound in the world of the tarantula, but most of those stories involve not the vicious, deadly or supernatural nature of the spider, but rather the ignorance that so often taints its care in captivity.

A young boy ties a string to a tarantula's leg to guide it around as though walking a dog. Cringe. A proud owner props a docile tarantula up on her shoulder as the perfect accessory to her Halloween witch costume. Danger. When it's time for a tarantula to molt, to shed its outgrown exoskeleton, a well-meaning owner provides his pet spider with a nice dry, very warm environment, just like it would have out in the desert it came from. No!

ABOUT THE TARANTULA

The fact is, not much is known about tarantulas in comparison to what we know about other more common pet species. They are rather mysterious

The Tarantula as a Pet

	Light	1	2	3	4	5	*Heavy*
TIME COMMITMENT			🕷				
MAINTENANCE Grooming		🕷					
Feeding				🕷			
General Clean-Up			🕷				
SUITABILITY TO CHILDREN Ages Infant-5		🕷					
Ages 5-10				🕷			
Over 10					🕷		
SOCIABILITY			🕷				
EXPENSE OF KEEPING			🕷				

spiders, some of whom are happiest when burrowed into the ground, others content to play in the branches of trees in tropical rainforests. Much is yet to be learned about their behavior and their habits in the wild, but those devoted to keeping them in captivity know that you do not tie a string to a tarantula's leg, that carrying them around in a position that can lead to a fall can be fatal and that, even if native to a dry environment, tarantulas require moisture, especially at molting time.

The tarantula is *not* the ideal pet for every household, or a cuddly plaything for the children. This shy, stunning spider *is* a quiet, undemanding pet whose true personality defies its menacing image. The tarantula can be a terrific pet for an owner with an affinity for legendary creatures—as long as that individual has the patience to learn what it takes to keep that creature alive.

The tarantula is an arachnid. An obvious fact, yes, but one that must be taken to heart. Its care requirements are quite different from what you might offer a dog, a cat or a goldfish. Acknowledge this, and you take the first positive step toward keeping the spider healthy; healthy spiders of some burrowing species have been known to live almost thirty years in captivity.

That longer-lived spider is, of course, the female of the species, for males are generally destined for lifespans woefully shorter than those of their mates

This is a female Goliath birdeater. Tarantulas have been known to live for thirty years in captivity; females live longer than males.
Michael A. Siino

(although some captive males have been known to take as long as ten years to reach maturity; not a bad record). As for their lifespans in the wild, that remains a mystery, though burrowing species tend to outlive their cousins in the trees, females outliving males in any species. The lifespan of those burrowing females continues to present a fascinating mystery. As tarantula expert Dr. Robert Gale Breene III, of the American Tarantula Society, has said, some might just be immortal.

Getting a Good Look

Male or female, the tarantula moves about on eight legs that lift its large bulbous abdomen off the ground. Its body is protected by a tough external skeleton, called an exoskeleton, that is shed, or molted, periodically as the spider grows. Most tarantula species are covered with coarse, dark hair-like structures. The spider's resulting hairy appearance not only makes the tarantula an ideal, though undeserved, character actor in horror films, but it can also serve as an effective line of defense.

Like iguanas, tarantulas typically cannot be sexed until they reach sexual maturity. At this time, following a molt, the observant owner will see on a male a small structure called a palpal bulb on the underside of the front leglike structure called the pedipalp. It may take a practiced eye to spot these. Other than that, females tend to be plumper, and in some species, even larger than the males—and typically longer lived as well. Find tarantula breeders through the American Tarantula Society (listed in Appendix) or at reptile shows.

The Tarantula's Defense Mechanisms

The tarantula's signature hairs, as highly sensitive appendages of the spider's nervous system, are actually bristlelike *setae*, some of which are sensitive to even minor disturbances in the air. But others, especially those on the abdomens of New World species, are shaped like tiny barbs that will successfully fend off the advances of parasites—or of handlers who do not observe proper protocol. The hairs come loose when touched, and many species may subsequently flick those loosened hairs with their legs at someone or something they deem a threat. In this sense, the hairs can prove more of an irritant to a handler than can the tarantula's bite.

Generally, tarantulas are not considered dangerously venomous to humans. While it would be preposterous to make broad proclamations about tarantulas and claim they apply to all of the more than 800 tarantula species worldwide, to date, good arachnologists have found little evidence of tarantulas posing a threat to our species. Any threat tarantulas might present would more likely be linked to the hypersensitivity of a particular handler to the minute amounts of venom in the tarantula's bite, or to the handler's inexperience in handling these spiders.

Some species, such as the Mexican redknee tarantula and the Chilean rose, are famous for their docility, while others are less patient with humans and ever-eager to bite. In general, however, it is humans who pose more of a threat to tarantulas than vice versa, for any spider may bite if frightened or mishandled.

WHAT CAN HURT A TARANTULA

The greatest threat to the tarantula is that its abdomen will rupture. Because of the vulnerable exoskeleton and its role in protecting the spider's abdomen, particularly the abdomen of a burrowing spider, handling tarantulas involves a great deal of risk when the handler is inexperienced. While most tree-dwelling tarantulas have evolved to run upside down, cling, climb and even jump from their arboreal perches when threatened, one fall to the ground for a burrowing species, and the abdomen can split, causing the spider to bleed to death, contract an infection or suffer fatal internal injuries.

The burrowing species, as those who choose to keep them as pets should respect, are classic ground dwellers who prefer to remain squarely rooted on *terra firma*, where they know instinctively that their precious abdomens will remain safe from impact-related injuries. Lift them carelessly into the air, and they may become frightened or stressed, bite the hand that feeds them and sustain that fatal fall.

CHOOSING A HEALTHY, HAIRY SPIDER

Should you begin to believe that perhaps a giant hairy spider is the ideal pet for your household, evaluate the reasons. These vary greatly between owners, some of whom are just basically fascinated by the scientific aspects of keeping and living with spiders; others view tarantula ownership as a means by which they can become more interesting to other people; and others keep these special arachnids because in seeing them day in and day out, they are transported to another part of the world where the spiders are huge, the vegetation a jungle (or a desert), and survival a battle between the fittest.

When it's time to choose a specimen for a pet, you must first decide what species will fit best into your household. Most of the 800 known species of tarantulas cannot be kept as pets because their behavior renders them unacceptable for that role, because they are too rare or difficult to breed or because it is illegal to keep them. Of those that can be kept, some are more docile and willing to be handled than others, and some are easier to care for.

Burrowing species are frequently kept as pets, some collected from the wild in certain regions of California, Texas and Arizona. This, however, is probably not the ideal place for obtaining a tarantula pet. Aside from the fact that if you crave a tropical species, you won't be finding one of those in your backyard in Arizona, captive-bred spiders are generally healthier and more likely than their wild cousins to be free of disease and parasites.

On the bright side, as tarantulas are becoming more popular as pets, and as arachnologists and spider breeders continue to unravel the secrets to their care and reproduction, more and more are being bred in captivity, thus providing a more readily available pool of superior tarantula pets.

When you find a store or breeder that carries the tarantula species of your choice (keep in mind that many species are mislabeled in pet stores), look for a tarantula with healthy, strong legs that are not curled in. The spider should be alert, and it should react to movement around it.

Pay particular attention to the abdomen. A scrunched, pinched abdomen can indicate dehydration and/or malnutrition; dehydration is the leading cause of death in tarantulas. A healthy tarantula has a plump, round abdomen free of wounds or damage. While one of these spiders may, with immediate and proper treatment, survive wounds to its legs, an abdominal wound is often fatal.

If hair seems to be missing from the abdomen, fear not, particularly if the spider is a New World species. The hairs of these spiders may just be missing as a result of the spiders' defense rituals of flicking hairs. Those missing hairs

A bald abdomen is not unusual in a tarantula, especially one that has been "throwing" bristles from its abdomen at would-be predators. *Michael A. Siino*

will usually grow back. The same applies to a tarantula with a missing leg. This, too, is common. If the site appears to have healed and is not bleeding, the tarantula may still be a good pet candidate, for it should regenerate the leg after a molt or two.

The female of the species, given her longer lifespan, is obviously the gender most owners prefer. Collect a wandering tarantula from the wild, and it will probably be a male. Males are more likely to be out in search of mates than are females, the latter of which spend most of their time safe and secluded underground. Of course that male pet will probably not live long, which further explains why you should shop around and choose a reputable source from which to purchase a tarantula. You want to be able to trust the personnel: first, to be able to differentiate between males and females because the signs are often quite subtle, and, second, to be honest with you about what you are being sold.

ACCEPTING THE RESPONSIBILITY

Learning all you can about tarantulas in general, and your species of choice in particular, and then implementing what you have learned, is the secret to keeping tarantulas healthy, content and long lived. The trouble is, as tarantula popularity increases and the species available expand, more and more faulty information is being circulated, resulting in far too many ailing and prematurely dead tarantulas.

What you must first acknowledge is the tarantula's natural living situation. While there is no evidence that a burrowing spider must burrow, you are welcome to provide the spider with a substrate in which it may do so, but you may then never see your pet again. Tree-dwelling species can also fare well without branches to climb, but they are far more interesting to watch within a high vertical enclosure that is furnished with branches. However you choose to outfit your tarantula's home, certain basics do apply.

Humidity is one such issue. Species native to arid and semi-arid regions of North America will require less moisture than those accustomed to the humid rainforests of South America, yet both do require moisture. Failing to provide them with that moisture will kill them.

These considerations play into the grand scheme that is responsible ownership. Only by pursuing this noble goal, can you help your tarantula live that possible thirty years or more that should be its destiny. Only this way can you join the quest to determine if these spiders really are immortal.

Tarantula's Do's and Don'ts.

Arm yourself with the following common sense "do's" and "don'ts" for the care and handling of tarantulas, and your mission has begun.

First, *don't* take the tarantula out on Halloween to frighten the neighbor kids or to accessorize a particular costume. *Don't* tie a string around a leg and try to lead the spider around; try this and you may just end up with a spider with a broken leg, dead from a massive hemorrhage. *Don't* release a pet tarantula back into the wild, especially if it is an exotic tropical species foreign to your local ecosystem.

Don't take the tarantula outside to show it off in public. This is bad public relations, just as it is when snake owners wrap their large serpents around their shoulders and go for a stroll. Those frightened of large hairy spiders will not be amused. Having the objects of their fear thrust in their faces in public may simply exacerbate anti-arachnid sentiments. Such forays can also lead to a fatal injury to the spider.

Don't allow children to handle the spider unsupervised. Better yet, advise many keepers, don't allow children, especially young children, to handle the spider at all. Children are more inclined to move with jarring, clumsy, or inadvertently heavy-handed actions that could cause the tarantula to bite, subsequently to be dropped and finally to be mortally wounded. Older children may also be a threat in that they may want to show off, to impress their friends with this big scary spider in their hands that is traditionally sent forth to destroy James Bond and any number of would-be movie heroes.

The "do's" are equally important. *Do* keep the tarantula securely confined in a habitat appropriate to its species. *Do* handle it carefully and not too often. *Do* allow the kids to watch the tarantula, to marvel at the way it moves, the way it lives. This is a positive way to help young people learn to respect the fascinating family of arachnids, and understanding is definitely something these oft-maligned creatures could use.

And finally, *do* get to know each tarantula as an individual. Even veteran keepers never cease to marvel at the individuality and personality tarantulas will express when kept in a properly maintained environment. Depending on species and individual, these spiders have been known to exhibit distinct behaviors, culinary likes and dislikes and reactions to handling. We don't usually expect that from a pet such as this.

HANDLE WITH CARE

TLC stands for tender, loving care, but when used in the context of tarantula keeping, it could easily be changed to TLH: tender loving handling.

Tarantulas may be large and furry, but they are not meant to be petted like a puppy or cuddled like a kitten. Frequent handling of tarantulas is generally not a good idea, but most of these spiders, especially when approached by someone experienced in this endeavor, will cooperate.

Tarantula handling must be pursued with the greatest of care for both the spider's safety and the owner's comfort. It is unwise to allow a tarantula to climb up one's arm to the shoulder, or to carry it to school for dramatic effect. While, as we have seen, the hair structures on some tarantulas can prove irritating when they come into contact with human skin, an argument even more powerful against gratuitous handling is the fact that such treatment can lead to severe and even fatal injury to the tarantula.

Whether approaching the spider out of necessity or recreation, the tarantula's safety must remain your primary concern. Beginners may thus feel more comfortable when first honing their handling skills to wear gloves, primarily to conquer any of their own insecurities about close contact with the spider. If, however, you cannot see yourself ever growing comfortable with this type of pet, perhaps you should consider another type of companion.

Because most tarantulas, especially North American species, will cooperate with handling, the simplest technique is usually the best. Approach the spider, tap its leg gently to announce your presence, then hold your hand out in front of it and gently tap it from behind as a hint to where you want it to go. More experienced handlers have mastered the technique of first tapping the leg as a warning, then simply lifting the spider into the air, carefully supporting its body in doing so. Regardless of the method you choose, move smoothly and gracefully, preventing the spider from accidentally hitting surrounding objects in the process that may injure a flailing leg.

There are several precautions you must take when and if you handle your tarantula. This owner knows his pet and lifts it by the abdomen with a swift, clean motion.
Michael A. Siino

If you intend to handle and hold the tarantula, do so over a forgivingly soft surface or flooring that will be less likely to lead to a breakage-causing impact should you accidentally drop your precious cargo. Increase the safety odds by sitting down when handling the spider and holding it over a table or some other surface.

Should Your Bug Bite

While it is rarely a problem, do be prepared for a bite. It can happen, and you must be sure that it does not trigger a natural dropping response on your part. The pain of a bite is usually minimal, yet this is a puncture wound, so it should be treated as such. Clean the site with soap and water and apply a little antibiotic ointment. Only if you experience signs of an allergic reaction should the wound be referred to a physician for treatment.

The spider may give fair warning before it bites, perhaps by tapping the intended victim first or displaying some other behavior unique to that individual tarantula. Some species even produce a hissing sound with two ridges on its body, called stridulating devices, that the spider rubs together. But such warnings or no, the results of a bite can actually prove to be most deadly to the tarantula, which may get dropped.

Because handling is directly related to injuries to tarantulas, it's a good idea to be prepared for such emergencies. If you do find yourself with an injured tarantula, you'll be thankful if you have thought ahead and collected liquid bandage solution, artificial skin, glue and, believe it not, nail polish hardener, for just such events. Although these can contain elements toxic to spiders, they have also been known to save tarantula lives by stopping the bleeding when applied to minor wounds, even abdominal wounds.

Bleeding is a definite concern considering how easily an unchecked wound can kill a tarantula. A leg injury, for instance, can bleed profusely, but you may be able to save the spider's life by removing the leg at the joint (or the spider may throw the leg itself; if it does, you may need to assist by grasping the leg firmly and completing the disconnection). This may stop the bleeding, as tarantula joints are designed to assist in this process naturally, and the leg should regenerate after a molt or two.

THE IDEAL TARANTULA DIET

The one time you are likely to see the tarantula express opinions is when the dinner bell rings. Hardly a vegetarian, the tarantula will consume only animal prey—and usually live prey, at that. Like a discriminating French gourmet, presentation is all-important to a hungry tarantula.

Although species and individual tastes may dictate otherwise, the staple diet of most tarantulas, and one proven to satisfy nutritional needs quite nicely, should be a diet consisting primarily of live crickets (readily available at pet supply stores), perhaps supplemented with live mealworms and other small insects. Some of these spiders have been known to take pieces of beef heart, hamburger and dead mice, but that, of course, is a matter of taste.

You can further throw some variety in the mix by offering occasional moths and beetles that you collect yourself. Large tarantulas may also express an interest in young "pinky" mice and even adult mice, both of which burrowing species may actually ingest in the wild, as well.

Whatever you happen to be feeding a tarantula, the items must not be too large for the spider to maneuver in its unusual, even gruesome, digestive process. The tarantula can ingest only liquid, so it must liquefy its food before it may consume it. With its mouth located in front of its sternum, it uses external limbs to position the prey for mastication. Digestive fluids flow from the mouth onto the securely held prey, after which the partially digested morsel can be drawn into the mouth, allowing the body to absorb the nutrients.

At the end of mealtime, non-liquefied elements are left behind, usually on the floor of the tarantula's enclosure in the form of a tarantula-made structure called a *bolus*. These remnants should be removed by the owner as part of routine maintenance. A pair of long forceps can come in handy for this, just as they can for placing the food in the enclosure in the first place.

A tarantula's nutrition may be further fortified by sprinkling food items with vitamin and mineral supplement powder. Recent evidence also suggests that feeding healthy, well-fed, well-hydrated crickets to a tarantula is probably healthier for the spider (and safer, in that it will protect the tarantula from being attacked by an aggressive and/or hungry cricket at feeding time). What you cannot afford are crickets or insects that have been contaminated by even trace amounts of insecticides, which can be extremely dangerous to sensitive tarantulas.

How and How Often to Feed

Only within a sufficiently warm environment, approximately 75 to 90 degrees Fahrenheit, will a tarantula be adequately stimulated to eat. A cool tarantula may lose interest in food. Most healthy tarantulas properly housed will thrive on two or three crickets a week, offered in one or two feeding sessions during that time period. Underweight tarantulas, evident in an abdomen that's not quite as plump as it should be, should be fed more frequently, about every other day or so.

When feeding, it is generally safest to place only one cricket or similar food item in the tarantula's enclosure at a time. If the spider seems uninterested in dining at the moment, remove the prey and try again later. The spider may be preparing to molt. Leaving a cricket loose in its enclosure for an extended period of time could prove dangerous to a molting or soon-to-be-molting tarantula, or even to a tarantula that just doesn't feel like eating at that particular time.

If, on the other hand, the tarantula is hungry and takes the cricket, you can place more crickets in the enclosure, even several at once, for the tarantula may just go ahead and masticate and ingest them in one large clump. Do keep an eye on the situation, however. You may need to remove the prey if the tarantula's appetite wanes.

BUILDING A SPIDER SHELTER

Most tarantula species kept as pets, including the popular burrowing tarantulas we find in the Americas, should be housed solo. Some tree species may be amenable to cohabitation, particularly the pinktoe tarantula, a tree species often kept in beautiful natural arboreal colonies as part of their owners' household decor, but there is risk in allowing this. The tarantulas may coexist well for weeks or even months; then one day, you wake up and find that only one is left.

With any tarantula species, if you choose to house two or more together, you will probably end up with only one in the end, and that one will probably be the larger of the original two.

The components of proper tarantula housing depend on the species being kept, but for all species, safety should be the number one concern. Some believe housing should simulate as closely as possible what the tarantula would experience in nature, whether that be desert or rainforest. But this may lead such individuals to design a habitat that is not as safe as it should be.

Despite what information there may be out there to the contrary these days, the safest habitat (and the simplest to obtain and maintain) for a burrowing tarantula is a plastic sweater box or shoe box with a snap-on top. Safety is inherent in this design because the walls of the box are low, the top can be securely fastened to the body of the box, it offers the owner easy access to the enclosure interior and it can be easily cleaned.

The low walls of the sweater box will help ensure that the tarantula does not climb the wall, as some can when housed in glass fish tanks. If they do so, the spiders can fall and sustain abdominal or leg injuries. Ideally, the height of the enclosure wall for a burrowing species should not far exceed the width of the spider's leg span.

Tarantulas should be housed individually. This is a selection of safe housing options for these hairy spiders. *Michael A. Siino*

That secure top, with holes punched in it for ventilation, is critical, for with enough momentum, a strong, healthy tarantula can push a loose lid off its enclosure and escape. While on one hand this is dangerous for the spider, on the other, it is doubtful that even the most devoted tarantula owner would care to find his or her pet unexpectedly burrowed into the sheets at bedtime.

Another mistake people make is propping a screen top on the enclosure, under which the spider may squeeze its legs, cut them and bleed to death. Even the screen itself can pose a threat, because the most common screen mesh size—that used for windows—can cause torn legs when appendages become stuck in the mesh. This would explain why many veteran keepers prefer that screen not be used at all, and why they continue to stress the beauty of the sweater box.

Other safe options include plastic jar-like containers, which are available in a variety of sizes and come equipped with a secure screw-on top (which also must be punctured for ventilation). Also available are commercial terrarium setups, which offer ample living space and may prove to be more aesthetically pleasing to some owners than a plastic jar or sweater box.

Deep glass fish tank setups are best reserved for tree species, which are not as prone as are terrestrial species to abdominal injuries caused by falling. For obvious reasons, tree-dwelling tarantulas are engineered for climbing. But of course these tree dwellers in a lovely simulated jungle environment will also require a secure top to their enclosure. Simply buy the top made for the particular tank you are using.

There is to date no evidence that tarantulas require any special lighting setups, and in fact, in the wild, a burrowing specimen may spend most of its life underground. Nevertheless, tarantulas should not be kept in complete darkness, but neither do they require heroic lighting measures.

Lighting can come in handy for providing the necessary heat within the enclosure, particularly by way of a heat-giving incandescent light source. If you choose to employ this heating method, the light must be either installed outside of the enclosure or, if positioned within the enclosure, encased in wire. Such measures will keep the light out of reach of the spider, which could be injured or burned by coming into direct contact with this live electrical source.

You may from time to time like to place the enclosure in an area where it will receive filtered natural sunlight. On the other hand, never place it in direct sunlight or near a heater, both of which have the power to dehydrate and kill the spider before its owner even realizes what has happened. There's a reason why, when in the wild, these animals burrow in the ground and hide in the trees when the sun is high. Sun worshippers they are not.

The tarantula dream home is completed with furnishings, primarily those in which the tarantula may hide and escape the prying eyes of observers. Lightweight cork bark, a flower pot turned over on its side or a commercially available cave will not only satisfy the shy spider's desire to hide, but also might make the enclosure a bit more attractive to the human eye. These items must, however, be planted firmly into the flooring material to prevent them from rolling over and injuring an active arachnid. You may wish to throw a toy in, as well. Some tarantulas have been known to play with empty toilet-paper rolls, while others have been known to try and use them as tools to remove loose lids from the tops of their enclosures.

Moisture and Temperature

Acknowledging their own limitations, tarantulas are inclined to remain hidden during the day, primarily to steer clear of predators, but also to help retain the hydration of their bodies. In captivity, then, they must also be assured sufficient moisture.

While dehydration is itself a serious risk, so is the practice of overmoisturizing a tarantula's habitat. An overabundance of moisture invites fungal problems and parasitic infestations.

Some tropical tree tarantulas require more moisture than do their ground-dwelling, burrowing cousins that are native to more arid, usually North American, environs, but all require some level of moisture. In his experience, Dr. Breene has found that a shallow water dish anchored securely in the flooring material (preferably vermiculite) should provide all the moisture most burrowing species require. Submerge a sponge in the dish when housing small spiders that might drown when attempting to take a drink directly from the dish.

The shallow dish can help humidify a tropical tree-dweller's home, as well. In some cases, with some spiders, you may need to supplement the humidity further with occasional mistings—more than you might ever need

Allowing a burrowing tarantula species to meander across one's hand or up one's arm can be dangerous, but an arboreal (tree) species, such as this Martinique red, is designed biologically to cling to the surfaces it climbs. It may also be housed safely in a glass aquarium, which can prove deadly to a burrowing species.
Michael A. Siino

A low-sided plastic sweater or shoe box carpeted with vermiculite and equipped with a hiding cave will help keep a pet tarantula safe and content.
Michael A. Siino

for a burrowing species, but not so often or so abundantly as to undermine the overall health and hygiene of the enclosure.

Air temperature, too, must be a concern given the role of warmth in the tarantula's metabolic processes. Tarantulas, depending on species, can fare well in temperatures ranging from about 75 to 90 degrees Fahrenheit. It is usually wisest to keep adults at the lower end of this spectrum to maintain steady metabolism, while immature spiders can be kept at the higher end to assist them in maturation.

Named by many veteran tarantula keepers as the best flooring material for tarantula enclosures is a substance called vermiculite. Appropriate for either burrowing or tree species, this material allows for burrowing, yet it also retains moisture. It can also be misted with a spray bottle to increase humidity (but sparingly, remember, sparingly). It is best to use vermiculite that is pea- or corn-sized. Smaller material can be ingested or inhaled, which can cause serious health problems to the resident tarantula.

Vermiculite can be used in any of the favored housing structures, i.e., sweater boxes, jars, etc. A thin layer of vermiculite will suffice for most enclosures and most species.

If your goal is to re-create a rainforest setting, you may want to explore other more elaborate flooring options, as well, such as peat moss (not as effective for burrowing species), sphagnum moss and orchid bark. Whatever you choose, it is probably best to avoid carpeting the enclosure with soil. While some keepers do, soil can contain disease-causing microorganisms that may contaminate both the environment and the spider.

Housekeeping Duties

The ease of keeping house for a tarantula is one reason why this particular pet has captured the attentions of those seeking a quiet, low-maintenance housemate.

As long as the spider's environment remains clean and free of mold, mites and parasites, its enclosure should require very little attention. You must, of course, remain ever vigilant in your evaluations of the flooring condition and the overall cleanliness of the tarantula's home, but, if it remains clean and dry, the flooring should require infrequent changings. The structure itself may require thorough cleaning and disinfection only about once a year or so.

If you are housing a tarantula in a plastic sweater or shoe box, or in a plastic jar container, you may clean and disinfect this easily (with the resident spider waiting in a temporary holding container, of course), or you may just want to replace it every year. If you prefer the cleaning and disinfecting route, which is certainly friendlier to the environment, make sure to rinse all chemical agents thoroughly from the structure to protect the extremely chemical-sensitive tarantula from exposure to such substances.

Cleanliness is critical because of the threat of mites, which will gladly make themselves at home within an unsanitary tarantula habitat and then hitch a ride on the tarantula itself. Such an infestation may be prevented by removing the mite-attracting bolus remains left in the wake of a tarantula's meal as soon as possible.

Feces should be removed regularly, too, as should soiled flooring material, which may be removed in total or partially as needed. Change the water in

This is a shed exoskeleton. When owners spot this in their pet's habitat, they sometimes think their spider has died or cloned itself.
Michael A. Siino

the water dish regularly and remove uneaten food items whenever the tarantula tells you through its inactivity that it's not hungry right now, thank you. Such vigilance will also prevent an infestation of ants, a mob of which can kill a tarantula if they attack *en masse*. Preventive measures are preferable to insecticides, which will often kill a sensitive tarantula more effectively than they will the pests you are targeting.

WHEN YOUR SPIDER MOLTS

Aside from the times in which it is forced to ride on its owner's shoulder, the most vulnerable time for the tarantula is when it molts. Tarantulas molt frequently when they are young and growing, perhaps as often as every month or so; less often, approximately once a year, when they reach adulthood. As adults, females outmolt males in frequency because of their longer lifespans.

When it molts, the tarantula sheds its external skeleton to make way for a new, larger one to develop and protect its body. Several days or weeks before molting, the spider will stop eating, and it may become lethargic. Refrain from placing food in the enclosure during this time. The spider may turn over on its back or onto its side. Resist those nagging suspicions that it must be dying, even though some definitely give that appearance. Eventually it will struggle out of the old exoskeleton, a new, larger spider ready to take on the world. Simple.

It's not so simple if the spider is not supplied with adequate humidity, a factor presumed to be the most common cause of molting problems and even molting-related deaths. This is especially true of tropical species, which can die during molting without plenty of moisture in the air. Facing great difficulty struggling out of its old shell, the spider may injure itself and quickly bleed to death. Easing the molting process, then, is a valiant goal.

Providing that all-important moisture, and possibly preventing an untimely tarantula death, is quite simple. If you have already been maintaining the appropriate humidity levels, this alone can help prevent problems. At the first sign of molting behavior, however, you may want to increase the mistings of the vermiculite until molting is complete, which should not take long. You may even mist the tarantula itself, but target only its legs and the upper side of its abdomen and body; if you saturate the book lungs underneath the tarantula, the spider could drown.

For the first few days after molting, the tarantula will remain vulnerable. During this time, do not handle the spider, and certainly do not feed it. This is one time in which the prey may turn on, and kill, the predator.

Molting is a very natural process that every tarantula must undergo. It should not, it need not, be a fatal one.

Within the eyes of the tortoise lies a mysterious and ancient wisdom. *Michael A. Siino*

CHAPTER 12

Slow and Steady Wins the Race: The Turtle and Tortoise

Thousands of years ago, a wise and rather creative Greek gentleman by the name of Aesop taught those gathered to hear his stories that slow and steady wins the race. He imparted this message to his listeners in a tale concerning a certain tortoise and a certain hare, who were pitted against each other in a race. In the end, though quite a bit slower than his long-eared opponent, it is the tortoise who wins. What he lacks in physical speed, we learn, he makes up for in superior diligence, wisdom and commitment.

Today, in an era where everything is fast—cars, computers, food—we still think fondly of old Aesop's fable. We still look with fascination upon the tortoise, and on its more aquatic cousin, the turtle. In these creatures, perhaps we see what we wish, however unrealistically, to aspire to ourselves.

At first glance, just as happened with the hare, the tortoise may appear to be an awkward, lumbering creature. Yet after that first glance, we find it difficult to look away.

Deeper concentration reveals an immensely graceful animal that seems to move within a frame of slow motion with calculated, determined action. We are flushed with a soothing sense of calm as we watch every well-planned step, every move of the head, and we are inspired by the wisdom that glows deep within the unabashed gaze of its eyes. Experience this and it is little wonder that a wise old soul such as this can so mesmerize, captivate and become not only a pet, but a lifelong member of the family.

Turtles and Tortoises as Pets

	Light	1	2	3	4	5	Heavy
TIME COMMITMENT				🐢			
MAINTENANCE Grooming			🐢				
Feeding					🐢		
General Clean-Up					🐢		
SUITABILITY TO CHILDREN Ages Infant-5	🐢						
Ages 5-10			🐢				
Over 10					🐢		
SOCIABILITY				🐢			
EXPENSE OF KEEPING				🐢			

MEET THE CHELONIANS

Turtles and tortoises as a group are known as chelonians. Although both require access to water, tortoises are considered to be basically terrestrial in their lifestyles, turtles more apt to be aquatic (some more than others). Still others, such as the box turtle, seem to stand in the middle.

If one of these creatures seems to hold you rapt within the wisdom of its gaze, that is probably for good reason. Chelonians have existed on this planet for an estimated 200 million years, traversing earth today essentially the same as they did in the beginning. Having shared the same terrain, the same watering holes, the same air as countless now-extinct animals of various eras passed, the chelonians may lay claim as witness to earth's history as few other creatures can, their survival standing as a testament to their victory as some of "the fittest" in the dangerous game of natural selection.

Yet the wisdom of the chelonians is apparent on an individual basis, as well. With wisdom comes age and some tortoises have been known to live 100 years or more. A fiftieth birthday for a California desert tortoise is probably just the halfway point for that animal, which should still be lumbering about long after most humans of its current acquaintance are gone.

But even though these animals have survived every natural disaster, every type of predator, every type of threat, it appears twentieth-century mankind may have finally figured out how to threaten the chelonians as no other danger ever has. Today a vast number of chelonian species are listed as endangered thanks to the devastation of worldwide habitat destruction, wanton treatment by humans and the demand for chelonian body parts by the illegal wildlife trade.

Because of their slow gaits and relative lack of protection against the mechanical toys of twentieth-century human predators, tortoises especially are frequently the victims of human cruelty. In California, for example, barbarians often choose the endangered California desert tortoise for target practice. Others are hit by cars or all-terrain vehicles, either by accident or intentionally. Despite such atrocities, these fates often bring the tortoises into the care of more compassionate humans.

While prospective pet owners must be careful not to choose an endangered animal as a pet, which may ultimately be confiscated, a special provision exists for the California desert tortoise. Because it is so frequently the

California desert tortoises are listed as endangered species and cannot be purchased or sold. They can only be kept as pets by people who rescue them and obtain state-issued permits. *Michael A. Siino*

target of abuse, a great many of these animals have been rescued and nursed back to health by families who go on to live quietly and contentedly with their beloved animals for decades. Acknowledging the efforts of these individuals, the state of California administers a permit program that allows these individuals to keep their pets, but this is the exception, not the rule. By law, you may not remove these animals from the wild, nor may you purchase or sell them. Period. And that applies to many other species of endangered tortoises and turtles, as well. (Permits for the keeping of rescued California desert tortoises can be obtained from the California Turtle and Tortoise Club, listed in the Appendix.)

WHICH TO CHOOSE?

The roster of the world's chelonian species is rich with names from all over the world. Most are endangered, and only a few of them are appropriate to keep as pets. While most of these are really not the ideal pet for beginning pet owners, especially for those with no previous experience with reptiles, even a beginner's strong commitment to their care can overcome that hurdle, after which these particular pets can become quite addictive.

At the beginning of the addiction, you are likely to notice that some species are far more readily available than others, which may in turn affect which you will choose.

Although opinions may vary on the subject, turtles are generally considered to be more inclined to spend time in the water, tortoises on land. One of the most popular turtle species actually seems to be part tortoise, as well. This is the **North American box turtle**, an animal that, like all chelonians, requires both shade and water, the latter of which is best provided in a flat container in which it may soak.

This popular species takes its name from its ability to close its shell up at each end, thus creating a box-like structure. When threatened, it retreats and battens down the hatches, closing both ends very tightly. Thus it remains safe inside until the danger has passed. Owners are to be warned, however, that if you get your finger caught in an end that is about to close, the pain can be intense, but you must be careful removing it so as not to injure the turtle.

Another popular pet turtle is the **red-eared slider**, so named for the red patches behind its eyes. This attractive aquatic turtle enjoys spending a great deal of time swimming in the water (unlike the box turtle, which merely soaks). Its pool of water should be maintained at about 75 to 86 degrees Fahrenheit. The red-eared slider must also have plenty of access to dry land and to an area where it may bask in the rays of either the sun or indoor full-spectrum lighting. With proper care, this attractive turtle should attain a shell size of about twelve inches.

The North American box turtle is a commonly kept pet. It takes its name from its ability to close its shell at both ends when threatened. *Michael A. Siino*

We find a much broader range of size in tortoises, as they, depending on species, may be only a few inches in size or weigh as much as 500 pounds. While some species enjoy the company of other tortoises, others are more content to live with humans than with other chelonians. These particular animals prefer being scratched under the chin and meandering around the garden alone, to spending time with a fellow tortoise.

Despite their positive pet characteristics, fewer tortoise species are available as pets. Many prospective owners prefer to choose a captive-bred tortoise in support of the endangered status so many of them are facing in the wild.

Many an experienced herpetologist further believes that it is best to choose a tortoise that, because of its native environment, is biologically accustomed to the type of area in which it will be kept in captivity. For example, a species native to the humid rainforests of South America, such as the yellow-footed tortoise, will thrive in equally humid regions such as Florida, while a species more accustomed to arid lands, such as the leopard tortoise, will find such a humid environment physiologically difficult, if not impossible, to adjust to.

Some tortoises are rather difficult to keep, so first-time owners are wise to stick with the easy keepers. Two that belong to this category are South America's **red-footed tortoise**, which hails from edges of humid forests and can grow to a foot in length or longer, and the **yellow-footed tortoise**, which typically averages about fourteen inches in length and is a species acclimated to forest life in South America. Both are very adaptable, fare well on a diet of fruit, vegetation and a bit of animal protein such as dry dog food thrown in for good measure and can tolerate various levels of humidity and air temperatures.

A species better acclimated to a drier environment is the **leopard tortoise** of central and southern Africa, which can weigh about sixty pounds and grow to about eighteen inches. Arizona may be a better home for this animal than Florida, for while the leopard tortoise may be somewhat tolerant of cooler temperatures, it cannot tolerate humidity.

Another tortoise you might find available as a pet is the **Southeast Asian elongated tortoise**, which should be about twelve inches long and weigh in at about ten to twelve pounds. This can be a more complicated species because it may require more animal protein in its diet than do most other species and it does not always take a liking to others of its kind. A species native to forested areas, it can tolerate humidity, but it prefers shade and the comfort of a secluded hiding place to long-term exposure to direct sunlight; it is thus less likely than are other species to spend a great deal of time basking.

More likely to be a basker is the **California desert tortoise**, a long-lived species that requires room to explore and graze; shelter from the sun when it finishes basking; and a healthy, primarily vegetarian diet. But of course such considerations are of concern only to those whom providence smiles upon and brings a California desert tortoise into their lives, as it is illegal to sell or purchase one.

LIFE WITH TURTLES AND TORTOISES

Although only a several-hundred-page encyclopedic-sized volume could adequately describe the detailed care required for every species of pet tortoise and turtle, some basics do apply to all. For one, pet turtles and tortoises, members of probably the most universally admired reptile group, can be very social pets, attentive to the goings on within their families, and interactive with family members. Yet they are often mistreated and sent on a path, generally fueled by ignorance, that robs them of the long lifespan that is their birthright.

The individual who takes the important step toward the commitment of keeping chelonians must learn about and respect these animals' special needs and meet them properly. A desert tortoise, for example, will require housing far different from that of a turtle that spends most of its time in the water.

While turtles and tortoises make excellent outdoor pets, whether providing indoor or outdoor accommodations, your goal is to simulate as best you can what they would be most accustomed to in the wild. They require water sources (size and depth dictated by species), shade, hiding places and basking areas. As with all reptiles, temperature is always a concern, and housing may need to change with the seasons to ensure the animal is kept adequately warm or cool, especially in winter when many a healthy pet chelonian hibernates. Provide for this incorrectly, and come spring you may no longer have a pet to care for.

The handling of chelonians may also defy your expectations. Yes, they move slowly relative to other types of pets, but steady as they are in their resolve, they can, as Aesop well knew, transport themselves from one spot to another with surprising speed and grace. Given that deceptive speed and their typically docile temperaments, newcomers to these unique pets may assume that handling a turtle or tortoise presents no challenge. Not so.

Aside from those tortoise species that are too massive to lift and carry, even a smaller chelonian can have surprisingly strong legs that it may push away with when held, almost as if it is swimming. Lift the animal by the shell, or carapace, so that its weight is distributed evenly on each side and prepare

Time spent outside in a safe enclosure lets a pet chelonian, like this red-footed tortoise, nibble on grass and enjoy basking in the sun. *Michael A. Siino*

for a push; otherwise you might drop the animal with dire results. Many an owner has also learned the hard way that a turtle or tortoise unaccustomed to handling or one that is stressed may bite or defecate without the least bit of warning. Surprise!

And finally, when committing to the keeping of a tortoise or a turtle, do the animal a favor and think of the future. Remember, many of these animals are quite long lived, some, tortoises especially, destined to outlive their owners. It's not unusual to see them passed down from generation to generation within families. In this light, the animals are truly members of the family, their rhythms acknowledged and accommodated as seriously as those of any two-legged member of the household. Those are the lucky tortoises.

When such inheritance arrangements are not possible, the animals may end up in rescue groups that consider placing homeless chelonians in new good homes to be a noble mission; others may end up in pet stores to find a new life through that avenue. The one option that must never be considered is releasing a pet chelonian back into the wild. Not only will the odds of its survival be dismal, it may transmit disease to other reptiles with whom it comes into contact. No reptile, wild or domestic, deserves such a fate.

EVALUATING AND NURTURING A HEALTHY CHELONIAN

The journey toward life with a chelonian begins with choosing a healthy animal. Not always as readily available as other reptile species, and plagued by all the typical health and nutritional problems that can affect reptile pets, turtles and tortoises are usually best purchased from breeders or from pet shops that specialize in reptiles.

Many species today are readily bred in captivity. This fact makes the choice of a particular animal simpler for those who believe captive-bred animals provide a more responsible option, and who believe that they make better pets because they are naturally adjusted to life with humans. The captive-bred animals also make healthier pets, less likely to be afflicted by disease and parasites. Wild-caught animals, for instance, are likely to be so stressed from capture that their compromised immune systems make them ripe for the onset of disease.

As knowledge regarding their reproduction has improved, captive-bred tortoises are now more readily available than ever before. Simultaneously, it is becoming more difficult to import them from the wild. Because habitat destruction is the primary cause of tortoise endangerment today, captive breeding efforts are seen by many as a blessing to pet owners and to the well-being of the animals as a whole.

When faced with choosing a pet that could be in your family for the next sixty, eighty, even one hundred years, choose a healthy looking animal with clean, clear, bright eyes and a hard shell. It should also appear relatively active and alert. Though it is typically a slow-moving animal on land, the healthy tortoise, for example, should walk with a jaunt in its step, lifting its body off the ground as it moves forward.

A poor appetite, listlessness, lack of activity, swollen eyes, a runny nose and open-mouth breathing are the classic signs of respiratory problems so prevalent in chelonians. Swollen eyes and/or a soft shell can be a sign that an animal is receiving an inadequate diet and/or is not getting enough sunlight. If you notice that the turtle or tortoise is not interested in food and has a whitish, almost furry, fuzzy appearance to the skin on the tongue and around the mouth, as well as a strong foul odor about the head, that animal probably has mouth rot (necrotic stomatitis), a common and extremely contagious bacterial infection that affects reptiles in general and chelonians, most often the terrestrial species, in particular. Look also for signs of infection on the shell or signs of diarrhea, the latter of which could indicate an infestation of internal parasites.

Fortunately, most illnesses in chelonians can be treated, assuming of course that treatment is begun right away and with assistance from a qualified veterinarian, of which more and more are emerging nationwide. Ill or injured turtles and tortoises that usually live outdoors should be brought indoors to prevent infection and to facilitate healing. No matter what you do, don't use guesswork in treating and caring for turtles and tortoises. What works for one species can kill another.

Illness in chelonians is most often the result of poor environmental hygiene, a lack of proper exposure to sunlight or ultraviolet lighting, stress (perhaps from the trauma of capture from the wild or from cohabiting with a larger, more dominant animal) or an improper diet. These conditions may occur within a pet household, but so may they also occur at a seller's facility. Although most medical conditions can be remedied with assistance from a veterinarian skilled in the care of reptiles, the animal suffering with them should be avoided when evaluating a new prospective pet.

Many chelonians can coexist with each other in captivity, but to prevent an outbreak of aggression, it is usually wise to keep males of some species with females rather than with other males. If keeping different species together, make sure the animals are of the same size and temperament, or there will be trouble, especially at feeding time. Quarantine is also critical, as newcomers should be kept separate from other chelonians and reptiles. The quarantine should be for as long as three months to prevent them from transmitting disease or parasites to the existing reptile population.

A SAFE STRUCTURE FOR A HOME

Tortoises and turtles are found all over the world. When designing where a pet chelonian will reside, consider its home environment and simulate it as best you can. Species native to North America, for example, will probably do well in many regions of the United States, while more foreign tropical species usually require higher temperatures and more humidity. Aquatic species will require water in which they may swim, while more arid species simply cannot abide high humidity in the air.

As with most reptiles, owners often become obsessed with the hobby of housing turtles and tortoises, seeing just how elaborate they can get in providing the most comfortable habitats possible. This mission is guided by what the animals would be accustomed to in the wild. This is usually a gradual process: You begin with a good basic setup that becomes more elaborate as you learn more about your pet and how best to provide for it.

While accommodations will vary from species to species depending on whether it is aquatic or arid in its acclimation, some basics do apply. For one, turtles and tortoises, as is common to reptiles, require warmth which may only be provided by external heat sources.

Although some species, such as the red-footed and yellow-footed tortoises, can tolerate somewhat lower temperatures at times, with the exception of hibernating season, most chelonian species flourish best in daytime temperatures that range from about 75 degrees Fahrenheit to the high 80s. A chilled chelonian, or one that must reside in an unsanitary environment, is a prime candidate for serious respiratory ailments that must be treated by a veterinarian. While proper warmth can prevent these, so will it stimulate the animal's appetite and help its body assimilate the nutrients from its diet.

Also like other reptiles, the turtle or tortoise should have options. Offered various temperatures within its enclosure, it should have the freedom to move from one temperature to another, or, for the outdoor animal, from the sun to the shade or hiding place. These options allow the animal to move from the warmer to the cooler areas and back again as needed. A turtle or tortoise living indoors, for example, may spend a great deal of time in a spot that is about 74 degrees Fahrenheit, but move occasionally to the spot on the other end of its habitat that is heated by an incandescent, heat-producing light to 85 to 90 degrees.

Housing designs are as varied as the species of chelonians. Some animals, such as red-eared sliders housed indoors, must have aquarium-style setups that are predominately water (clean water) but that do include an ample island of rock or other "land" for basking. Others, such as a desert tortoise or a box turtle, will require secure footing and only a minimum of water for drinking or soaking. These animals' water may be easily provided in the bottom section of a flower pot filled just high enough to cover the bottoms of their shells should they decide to take a soak (too high, and the animal can drown).

Most turtles and tortoises do well, even best, when they are allowed to live outdoors in the backyard when the weather is warm enough for them to do so. It's not unusual for chelonians in Florida and other southern realms to remain in outdoor accommodations almost all year long. This is satisfactory as long as during cooler times they are offered bedding more appropriate for winter, such as thick piles of leaves or mulch. Some species will hibernate (see "A Long Winter's Nap," p. 204); those that don't may require an outdoor heated sleeping box to which they may retreat for that much-needed warmth. Still others may live part of the year outdoors and part of the year indoors when the weather becomes too harsh (see "Keeping Your Chelonian Outdoors," p. 200).

When kept indoors, the habitat of the turtle and tortoise must closely resemble what the animals would enjoy outdoors. In addition to a clean environment, a variegated diet and fresh water, another important requirement is lighting, for the indoor animal will not have access to sunlight.

Overhead full-spectrum lighting is what you are seeking. This is offered most easily in a fluorescent light. In substituting for the sun, this lighting provides the animal with the specific rays it needs to enjoy a healthy appetite and the metabolic benefits of ultraviolet light. Supplement this with an overhead incandescent heat-producing bulb at one end of the enclosure, which will provide the warmth the animal will seek for basking. Turn the lights on for about twelve hours a day to mimic daytime.

If you truly want to keep your indoor tortoise or turtle healthy and content, why not take it outside from time to time to let it soak up a little sun? This does not mean placing it in a glass aquarium or forcing any direct exposure to sunlight, which can be deadly. Rather, under close supervision, and obviously within an escape-proof yard or enclosure, allow the animal to browse around, perhaps catch an insect or two for a treat and nibble on the dandelions, bask in the sun and then move into the shade. In planning such an outing, avoid the temptation to tether the animal to keep it from wandering. As horrific as it sounds, there are some who have tied a string to a leg or tied a rope through a hole drilled in the shell for just that purpose. Despite the convenience they promise, never even consider such cruel actions.

Interior Decorating

Whether the animal is living indoors or out in an aquarium, a commercially purchased terrarium, a wooden enclosure made of boards or a big backyard, a chelonian's habitat must be escape-proof. Within the confines of this habitat should be a shelter, a basking spot and an appropriately sized water source.

Most privacy-loving chelonians also require hiding places where they can retreat from both prying eyes and light.

For chelonians that are more terrestrial than aquatic, the type of flooring you choose is critical. While the flooring of an outdoor enclosure can ideally be natural grass, an indoor enclosure should be carpeted with such safe materials as newspaper, peat moss or indoor/outdoor carpeting. Disposable flooring material should be changed completely every week, and partially as it becomes soiled with feces, urine and food remains. Carpeting, too, must be cleaned on a regular basis.

For terrestrial species, shredded newspaper is an excellent flooring choice, pleasing to both the tortoise that enjoys burrowing (and many do) and the owner who appreciates a material that is so easily removed and replaced. While clean gravel may be fine for the floor of a predominantly aquatic setup, avoid using gravel, as well as sand, dirt, ground corn cobs or wood shavings, as a substrate in a more terrestrial animal's lair. The turtle or tortoise might ingest the stuff, especially, say, sand that sticks to its food, and it will consequently become quite ill.

Wood products are inappropriate because they can be dehydrating, and wood chips can injure the eyes of a reptile attempting to burrow. Dirt or soil, aside from the cleanliness factor, can contain microorganisms dangerous to the animal. Peat moss, on the other hand, is relatively cleaner, and it can be spritzed with a mister to keep it moist. A hill of the moss constructed within the enclosure can be an attractive substrate for a burrowing tortoise or box turtle.

Of course no tortoise or turtle habitat is complete without water, which, as we've seen, must be provided as befits the individual species' needs. For the non-swimming chelonian species, such as the box turtle, water can be provided within an appropriately sized plastic, stainless steel or ceramic dish. This, like all furnishings within the enclosure, should be embedded in the tank substrate, making it more easily accessible to the turtle or tortoise and less likely to be tipped over. The water, whether provided for drinking or soaking, must be fresh and clean, preferably changed on a daily basis.

KEEPING YOUR CHELONIAN OUTDOORS

As we have seen, in some areas, turtles and tortoises are most content when allowed to live in outdoor accommodations all or part of the year, with access to indoor options when the weather turns mean. By the same token, some owners prefer to keep their pets indoors at night and outdoors during the day. Either way, the weather must be appropriate for the protection of these reptiles that require adequate warmth.

If given their druthers, adult tortoises, for example, usually fare best outdoors where they can wander around, nibble the grass, hibiscus flowers and dandelions, and get plenty of exercise and sunshine. If this is what you hope to provide for your pet, three safety requirements must be met: The enclosure or yard must be escape-proof; the area must not be treated with pesticides or fertilizers; and the animal must not be allowed access to a swimming pool. In this latter case, terrestrial species can drown, while aquatic species can become trapped in the pool filter.

Some distinct benefits of housing chelonians outdoors is that they do not need special lighting for they will reap the benefits of the sun, the ultimate reptile light source, nor may they require heavy supplementation of vitamin D3 that is so critical for indoor reptiles. Despite the benefits of the sun, however, the animals must have access to shade at all times, as well as to water for soaking, drinking and, for the aquatic species, swimming.

While many terrestrial species, with diligent supervision, can wander the yard unrestrained in search of vegetation and bugs on which to nibble, designing appropriate outdoor accommodations that will sufficiently house these animals on a more long-term basis is really quite simple.

For a tortoise or box turtle, begin by building a sturdy, secure pen; untreated wooden boards are ideal for this. Make sure the pen is escape-proof by making the walls high enough (twice the length of the tortoise) to prevent a climbing escape and well anchored to the ground to prevent a burrowing escape. Though box turtles, for example, enjoy life outdoors, they need an extra-strength pen that will withstand their attempts to dig underneath or to climb over with the help of plants positioned close to the pen walls.

Security is critical, as stories abound of tortoises and box turtles found meandering down an urban street or munching flowers in a garden. Most of these were either lost or abandoned pets. The outdoor pen setup will help prevent you from losing a much-loved pet while providing the animal with the benefits of the great outdoors. If one does wander away, it may be taken in by someone who is not willing and/or able to care for it properly; it may ultimately end up injured or killed.

Construct the terrestrial animal's pen on a patch of grass, preferably surrounding other types of vegetation such as dandelions and hibiscus flowers (favorite tortoise treats). Furnish this with the hiding box (an appropriately sized wooden box or hollowed log for smaller animals, a plastic igloo-style or traditional doghouse for larger individuals); the water dish; a large flat rock, brick or cement slab for basking; and perhaps a pile of leaves for burrowing. Make sure there is plenty of shade, and you're in business.

For the aquatic turtle's outdoor habitat you will need the same pen, only this time place a child's pool filled with water in the middle, and position a large flat rock or concrete block securely in the center, upon which the turtle can climb to bask in the sun. Of course, one section of this pen must be shaded, as well.

These simple setups provide the animals with any type of activity they might desire: all have access to sunshine and shade, and terrestrial animals have access to vegetation on which to graze. So housed, turtles and tortoises can soak up all that good fresh air and sun to their heart's delight. You must check them regularly to make sure they are safe, still there and have not fallen on their backs, which can happen when, in the universal belief that the grass is always greener, they try to climb the pen wall in a daring escape attempt.

And finally, remember that indoor turtles and tortoises, too, would just love a romp in the yard from time to time. You don't have to house them out there full-time, but do allow them some of the benefits when you can.

FEEDING YOUR TURTLE OR TORTOISE

Turtles and tortoises are typically painted as classic vegetarians, but that notion is not necessarily accurate. Yes, they gladly partake of fruits and vegetables, they will gladly partake of food in general because they do love to eat, but they should more accurately be described as omnivores: eaters of both meat and vegetation.

On their own, turtles and tortoises naturally ingest animal protein in the form of insects or other invertebrates; in captivity, they even take high-quality dog food when it is offered. The lesson to be learned here is that a variety of foods in the diet will provide the full complement of nutrients so vital to the healthy tortoise and turtle.

Another truth about these animals is that they are known for large appetites, more pronounced in the young than in adults. Either way, they should be fed every day. They are delightful to watch as they munch with as much gusto as a chelonian is capable of expressing. Despite that often voracious appetite, however, do avoid the temptation to overfeed.

That appetite and that gusto rely heavily on the warmth of the animal's body. Too cool, and it probably will not eat. Properly warmed, however, the animal can enjoy a variety of foods, the mix of which is rooted in what the animal would likely find in its native habitat. Learn all you can about your pet's natural diet in the wild and let that be your guide. Carefully monitor its health, as well, which will tell you what you need to know about the diet's effects.

While there is no way to prescribe one list of foods that are ideal for every species of turtle and tortoise, most terrestrial species enjoy such bulky fruits and veggies as squash, apples, dandelion greens, plums, tomatoes, cantaloupe, strawberries and okra. For obvious reasons, tropical species usually exhibit

A diet of fresh fruit and vegetables, perhaps supplemented with occasional animal protein, will satisfy a chelonian's very healthy appetite. *Michael A. Siino*

more of a liking for fruits than do their North American counterparts. But with all species, take it easy with the green leafy vegetables; spinach, cabbage and nutritionally sparse iceberg lettuce can cause digestive upset. Choose escarole, collard greens or romaine lettuce over these, and feed them sparingly.

Monitor the animal daily for any sudden changes in appetite, and examine its feces for changes in consistency. For instance, you don't want to provide your chelonian pet with a diet that is too wet (as can happen when it is too rich in tomatoes), which will be evident in feces that are wet and loose rather than firm and compact.

Most of these animals also thrive with a supplement of animal protein to their basically vegetarian diets. Animal-based protein contains amino acids, critical components in the maintenance of those beautiful shells. You can provide the box turtle and many tortoise species with these proteins in the form of light commercial dog food, night crawlers, slugs, snails or crickets that are not contaminated by pesticides. The turtle or tortoise allowed outdoors may even find some of these latter items on its own while exploring the vegetation in the backyard.

Special treats—and a special nutrition-related activity—may be provided by allowing land-dwelling turtles or tortoises to explore the backyard and/or garden (in secure confinement and supervision). These animals love nothing more than to move along with that special grace of theirs in search of the perfect patch of lawn on which to nibble, and perhaps a dandelion or two. Hibiscus flowers are similar favorites, but make sure that they, and any domestic vegetation your pets find, have not been tainted by pesticides.

Aquatic turtles, most of which must be fed in the water, have a different set of nutritional requirements. Their diets may include fish, lean beef, brine shrimp, night crawlers, Trout Chow and feeder goldfish, all obtained from a reputable source where you can trust the live food items to be free of bacteria or similar contamination. You, as owner, are also charged with preventing contamination, a mission accomplished by removing any uneaten food from the water and enclosure as soon as the turtle has made it clear it has had its fill. It might be easiest, therefore, to feed the water-loving animal in a smaller enclosure to keep the main habitat clean.

Like their terrestrial cousins, aquatic turtles, such as red-eared sliders, may also enjoy leafy vegetables and pulpy fruits, such as bananas and papayas. But to owners seeking variety in their pets' diets, a word of warning is provided by the California Turtle and Tortoise Club: Do not feed these turtles ant eggs. Once popularly recommended by those who didn't know better, these have been the downfall of too many turtles through the years.

Although their diets may differ between species, what is standard for all chelonians is the importance of vitamin D3 and calcium. Young growing animals require more calcium and protein for shell maintenance than do their elders, but these elements are critical for chelonians of all ages.

Supplementing the diet with a commercially available vitamin/mineral supplement is an intelligent step to take when caring for reptiles. The most convenient form is a powder formulated specifically for reptiles (meaning it contains vitamin D3) that can be sprinkled onto the animal's food. Because the turtle's and tortoise's diet is so rich in moist fruit and vegetable items, the powder will stick well.

Supplements are critical, but don't overdo it. Excess nutrition can be just as dangerous as malnutrition. Supplementing the meals once or twice a week should be all that is required for most turtles and tortoises.

A LONG WINTER'S NAP

If you thought bears were the only animals that enjoy a long nap when the weather turns cold, think again. Many species of turtles and tortoises enjoy a winter snooze themselves, but an owner must be cautious in allowing this.

Hibernation is healthy because the rest can help rejuvenate the animal, enhancing its health and well-being all year round. But not all chelonians hibernate (most of the more tropical species should not). Beyond that, it is an activity that must be reserved only for the healthiest animals; a sick or injured animal allowed to hibernate will suffer a terrible physical toll, and it may not wake up in spring. The ideal hibernation candidate is an animal that is at the peak of health and has been extremely well fed.

Of course, the owner plays a critical role in successful hibernation, as well: first in supplying the animal with a healthy diet, second in learning to recognize the signs of impending slumber and third in providing the animal with a hibernation place that will be safe, secluded and quiet.

To hibernate or not to hibernate is a very personal question, often dictated more by a chelonian's day-to-day living situation than by anything else. An outdoor tortoise, for example, is more inclined to hibernate than is an indoor animal. The cooling temperatures and shortened daylight hours will trigger instinctive responses in the outdoor animal that its indoor counterpart may never sense.

Consider, for example, the California desert tortoise and the box turtle. When fall arrives, they must be well fed, but watch for the telltale signs of impending hibernation: a loss of appetite, restlessness and sluggish behavior. The animal may begin to roam around looking for a sheltered spot and hover around a particular area. An indoor pet interested in hibernating will exhibit these same signs, and it, too, may hibernate if it is healthy. If you and your indoor pet both agree that hibernation is a good idea, gradually lower the temperature in its terrarium until it reaches about 65 degrees Fahrenheit and move it into a hibernation box as described below.

The thought of agreeing with a turtle or tortoise about hibernation may sound humorous, but it is serious business. You must never allow a sick or otherwise weakened animal to hibernate, for as its metabolism slows down, the animal could die. Remember too, that young chelonians usually do not hibernate. They really don't need to, and they probably won't even try.

Where the animal hibernates is the next concern. While many a keeper is comfortable hibernating these animals outdoors, this may occur only where outdoor winter temperatures average about 38 to 52 degrees Fahrenheit. If the mercury typically falls below freezing in your area, bring the animal in for its winter's nap. Allow a tortoise to hibernate outdoors during a Minnesota, New York or Colorado winter, and that will be the last you see that animal alive.

Fortunately, hibernation options do exist. The first is the outdoor option. Some animals will pursue this themselves—an aquatic turtle or a box turtle, for example, may seek out its own sleeping place, usually burrowing into a sheltered pile of leaves or similar vegetation in the yard. Offer a hint by building stacks of hay or bark in the yard where you would like the animal to hibernate. If you deem your pet's chosen spot acceptable, once the animal has dug in, cover the exposed top of its shell with hay, leaves or bark for further insulation, mark the spot clearly and check on the animal periodically throughout the winter to make sure it remains properly protected from the elements.

Because of the risk of floods, cold snaps and other unexpected dangers in winter, a better, safer outdoor alternative is to provide the animal with your own homemade sleeping quarters. A dog house is ideal for this, either a traditional model or, easier still, an igloo-style house that is sturdy and easily cleaned. Whether you choose a traditional style or an igloo, the house must be watertight to protect the animal from becoming wet or chilled. It should sit elevated off the ground to protect against the cold of cement or earth, the floor insulated with newspaper, straw or leaves to further keep the cold under control.

In areas where it is too cold to allow outdoor hibernation, or if you have an indoor pet that wants to hibernate, you can use this same dog house technique in the garage. In this case, a high-sided cardboard box will also suffice, but it too must be elevated off the cold cement and insulated with newspaper or straw.

If you choose a garage locale, make sure that the box or doghouse is located out of drafts, the garage is free of rats and that cars with their toxic fumes will not be started within the animal's vicinity while it sleeps. In most cases, indoor hibernation within the main household itself is unacceptable because the temperatures are too warm, but a cool closet in the garage or basement provides an alternative spot where the animal can remain unmolested from children and other animals. Label the box or house as a hibernation haven and record the date hibernation begins.

The turtle or tortoise who doesn't hibernate, either because its health doesn't warrant it or because its indoor lifestyle doesn't spark the instinct, will also require some special attention. Keep feeding these animals well, and make sure their environment, either indoor or outdoor, remains clean, properly lighted and warmed.

An outdoor animal that won't be hibernating may need to be brought indoors due to cold outdoor temperatures. It will still require a sturdy enclosure that offers a heat gradient ranging from about 75 to 88 degrees Fahrenheit (the latter being the basking area). Allow plenty of room for exercise, and do all you can to prevent stress and the commensurate health problems it can spawn.

SPRING WAKE-UP CALL

A turtle's or tortoise's hibernation does not mean you may forget about the animal for a few months while it slumbers. This animal too requires regular attention, in that you must check it constantly to make sure it remains properly protected and asleep.

For example, if an unexpected warming trend sets in, this may signal the hibernating chelonian to awaken. You will need to be alert to the stirrings of a prematurely awakening animal and do what you can to urge it back to

The difference between the male (left) and female (right) Texas tortoise is the male's concave underside and the female's flat underside, designed to facilitate breeding.
Michael A. Siino

sleep. This can be especially dangerous if a warming trend is followed by an equally sudden and extreme cold snap. Either way, if a turtle or tortoise awakens mid-hibernation and refuses to go back to sleep, you will need to provide it with the appropriate indoor accommodations so it may live out the rest of the winter safely.

When the time truly does come for awakening, usually in March or April, evident in the consistently warming temperatures outdoors that gently urge the animal to open its eyes, listen for stirrings within the hibernation place. Allow the animal to awaken fully on its own, then remove it and place it in a safe enclosure for post-hibernation rehabilitation.

During hibernation, turtles and tortoises lose a great deal of weight, primarily from water loss. Your goal now is to help the animal rehydrate and rebuild itself nutritionally. You can help a box turtle or tortoise in this by allowing it to soak for fifteen minutes at a time in about two inches of 75-degree water. When its body warms up a bit, it will feel more inclined to eat.

The newly hibernated turtle or tortoise may not feel hungry for a few days or even weeks, often until it has been fully rehydrated through drinking and soaking, but it should nevertheless appear healthy, active and alert. One that doesn't may be suffering from an onset of respiratory, eye or mouth problems that are fostered by the vulnerable condition caused by the slowed metabolism of hibernation. If this is the case, call the veterinarian, who may need to administer antibiotics or prescribe some other special treatment that will get the animal back on the road to health.

Allow the animal plenty of access to water for drinking and soaking during those first few weeks. When it regains its appetite (which some do right away), provide it with feasts of appropriate vegetables, fruits (rich in hydrating moisture) and animal protein (dog food, night crawlers, etc.). And don't forget those vitamin and mineral supplements so critical to shell strength and overall metabolic health.

Introduce the normal routine and access to sunshine gradually, all the while remembering that this is an extremely vulnerable, recuperative time for the animal. The healthy turtle or tortoise should appear enthusiastic and lively if not as physically energetic as you are accustomed to seeing it. Within about two weeks, you should all be back to the normal routine.

SALMONELLA AND CHELONIANS

No treatise on turtles and tortoises would be complete without a discussion about the "S" word: salmonella.

Only a few decades ago, one could be shopping in the local dime store, as it was called then, and in the midst of picking up some unplanned bargains you could buy a small turtle or two as well. Most of those small turtles would be dead within weeks if not days of their purchase. Their impetuous owners, not to mention the public at large, didn't know the first thing about proper turtle care, which, as we have seen, can be extremely complex.

These young red-eared sliders may be sold only when they grow larger than four inches to prevent the spread of salmonella among young children. *Michael A. Siino*

Then one day, those who studied such things discovered a connection between these small turtles and a great many cases in humans of salmonella, a debilitating intestinal bacterial disease that can be transmitted by reptiles (and other animals) to humans. Turtles and tortoises were immediately, and in part accurately, targeted as carriers of the disease, an accusation which led to legislation that prohibits the sale of any turtle or tortoise whose shell is less than four inches. The reason given for that seemingly arbitrary measurement was that a child, the most common victim of severe cases of salmonella, presumably could not place a four-inch turtle or tortoise in his or her mouth.

While this legislation failed to take into account the fact that salmonella could just as easily be transmitted when a child put a contaminated finger in his or her mouth after touching an affected turtle, it ended up beneficial for the turtles as well as for the children. No longer can people impulsively pick up a cute, inexpensive little turtle or two at the local drug store or pet shop, which would subsequently perish from malnutrition, dehydration or overexposure to the sun.

Yet even though those turtles are now off the market, salmonella remains a concern, especially now that we have discovered other carriers, such as the immensely popular green iguana and even the meat and eggs we buy at the grocery store.

While a turtle or tortoise affected with salmonella will itself show few, if any, signs of illness, humans who contract the disease become quite ill. This can be especially dangerous for the elderly, young children and anyone with a compromised immune system. This risk does not mean one should forego chelonian ownership; it just prescribes the need to follow some preventive measures to ensure that you and your family don't become infected.

These precautions are quite simple: Wash your hands before and after handling turtles, tortoises or any reptile pet, and do not allow the animal to come into contact with food preparation areas in the kitchen or similarly sensitive areas in the bathroom. Follow these simple tenets, and you may all live happily ever after for years, if not decades, to come.

APPENDIX

The following is a list of organizations enthusiasts may consult should they seek further information or the camaraderie of kindred spirits in the keeping of more unusual pet species.

Ferrets

California Domestic Ferret Association
P.O. Box 21040
Castro Valley, CA 94546

Central Arizona Ferret Club
4656 E. Glenrosa Avenue
Phoenix, AZ 85018

Ferrets Anonymous (working to legalize ferrets in California)
P.O. Box 3395
San Diego, CA 92163

Western New York & Finger Lakes Ferret Association
296 Benton Street
Rochester, NY 14620-2017

Hedgehogs

North American Hedgehog Association
601 Tijeras Avenue NW, Suite 201
Albuquerque, NM 87102

Iguanas

The International Iguana Society
Department of Biology
Southern College
Collegedale, TN 37315

Miniature Potbellied Pigs

National Committees on Potbellied Pigs
P.O. Box 2282
Oakhurst, CA 93644

North American Potbellied Pig Association
Austin, TX 78709-0816

Southern California Association of Miniature Potbellied Pigs
P.O. Box 8638
Riverside, CA 92515

Rats and Mice

*American Fancy Rat and Mouse
Association*
9230 64th Street
Riverside, CA 92509

*American Rat, Mouse and Hamster
Society*
9370 Adlai Road
Lakeside, CA 92040-4834

The Rat Fan Club
857 Lindo Lane
Chico, CA 95973

Reptiles and Amphibians

*American Federation
of Herpetoculturists*
P.O. Box 300067
Escondido, CA 92030-0067

Amphibian and Reptile Conservation
2255 N. University Parkway,
Suite 15
Provo, UT 84604-7506

*California Herpetoculture Industry
Advisory Council*
8459 Lakeland Drive
Granite Bay, CA 95746

Cedar Hill Enterprises
(regular sponsors of reptile
shows in the West)
3442 Primrose Avenue
Santa Rosa, CA 95407

Central Florida Herpetological Society
P.O. Box 3277
Winter Haven, FL 33881

Georgia Herpetological Society
P.O. Box 464778
Lawrenceville, GA 30246

Long Island Herpetological Society
476 N. Ontario Avenue
Lindenhurst, NY 11757

*The Maryland Herpetological
Society*
2643 N. Charles Street
Baltimore, MD 21218-4590

Michigan Society of Herpetologists
P.O. Box 13037
Lansing, MI 48901-3037

New York Herpetological Society
P.O. Box 1245
New York, NY 10163-1245

Ontario Herpetological Society
P.O. Box 244
Port Credit, Ontario L5G 4L8
Canada

Philadelphia Herpetological Society
3059 Unruh Street
Philadelphia, PA 19149-2500

The Pittsburgh Herpetological Society
Pittsburgh Zoo
Reptile Department
1 Hill Road
Pittsburgh, PA 15206

*The Southwestern Herpetologists
Society*
P.O. Box 7469
Van Nuys, CA 91409
or
P.O. Box 3881
Santa Barbara, CA 93130

Toledo Herpetological Society
1587 Jermain Drive
Toledo, OH 43606

Tarantulas

American Tarantula Society
P.O. Box 3594
South Padre Island, TX 78597

Turtles and Tortoises

California Turtle and Tortoise Club
P.O. Box 7300
Van Nuys, CA 91409-7300

New York Turtle and Tortoise Society
P.O. Box 878
Orange, NJ 07051-0878